What people are saying about

Crystals for Your Inner Goddess

Elina's work is always of an incredibly high standard, and I feel there is such a growing demand for information on crystals that it would be a popular choice for readers. Empowering, uplifting and beautifully written — this book is a must-read for any woman on a spiritual path.

Tanaaz Chubb, author of *The Power of Positive Energy* and owner of ForeverConscious.com

T0103417

Acknowledgements

We are grateful to our patients who gave us the opportunity to understand the experience of tinnitus. Thanks to their openness and honesty during the therapy sessions, we could see the problem from their eyes, put ourselves in their shoes and understand the difficulties they face because of tinnitus and its associated distress and anxiety. It was only through supporting our patients and reflecting on their feedback that we could develop techniques and management strategies that could help them in their individual journey of recovery from tinnitus distress. Here is what we give in return, a ten-step self-management guide to living well with tinnitus. The guide can be used by those who experience distressing tinnitus anywhere in the world.

This book is the result of many years of interactions with multiple groups of colleagues whose ideas, experiences and reflections have significantly contributed to the development and refinement of the methods presented here. First and foremost are the staff of the Tinnitus and Hyperacusis Therapy Specialist Clinic, Audiology Department, Royal Surrey NHS Foundation Trust, Guildford, UK, where Hashir Aazh had the privilege of serving as the Tinnitus Team-Lead for just over a decade (2010–2021). Our colleagues in Guildford have utilised many of the concepts presented here in their day-to-day clinical practice, and they have offered their reflections on practical aspects of therapy and evaluated and communicated their patients' experiences of receiving the treatment. So, it is fair to say that many of the ideas presented in this book originated from the colleagues listed here: Jills Kurian, Jemma Hatton, Jennifer Whiffin, Viveka Owen and Jenni Stevens. We are indebted to them.

In this book, we have pooled ideas from authorities in modern psychology who have pioneered methods for treating psychological and behavioural disorders. Their ideas and methods have been adopted in this book for the purpose of managing tinnitus-related distress. We are grateful for the wealth of knowledge created by these pioneers. Here, we list only the most prominent of these people: Jonathan S. Abramowitz, Judith S. Beck, James Bennett-Levy, Dennis Greenberger, William R. Miller, Christine Padesky and Stephen Rollnick. We also extend our gratitude to our colleagues and teachers in the field of tinnitus and audiology: David Baguley, Ali Danesh, Jonathan Hazell, Pawel and Margaret Jastreboff, Don McFerran, Laurence McKenna, Ahmadreza Nazeri, Deepak Prasher, Richard Salvi, Jacqueline Sheldrake, Robert Sweetow and Richard Tyler. The aim of this book was not only to adopt the methods of cognitive behavioural therapy (CBT), but to refine them and perhaps introduce new variations that in the future could be used in the treatment of other conditions that may benefit from CBT. To this end, although this book remains faithful to the theoretical underpinnings of CBT, it offers new metaphors, procedures and concepts that extend the scope of CBT in dealing with tinnitus-related distress.

We thank the following for helpful comments on an earlier version of this book: Robert Sweetow, Rory Allott, Kate Harvey, Jemma Hatton, Alan Hopkirk, Tine Roanna Luyten, Andrew McAleer, Estelle Novella, Maureen L Whittal and four of Hashir's former tinnitus patients. We thank Lika Kvirikashvili for drawing many of the illustrative figures used in this book.

Finally, it is important to acknowledge that the COVID-19 pandemic and solitary experiences during the national lock-down were a catalyst for putting together the materials that we have gathered over many years. Using video calls on a large scale as a substitute for face-to-face care for our patients made it clearer to us that there is an urgent need for evidence-based self-help materials that can be used by patients when there is limited access to clinical care. Given that self-help materials are easy to access, while visiting a doctor has become more difficult, the use of self-help materials is likely to grow in the future well after the pandemic has subsided. Finally, we can't resist referring to an article by Andrew Dickson published in the *Guardian* at the beginning of the UK COVID-19 lockdown. He suggested that William Shakespeare wrote *King Lear* during the plague quarantine in London! Although we can't claim that our writing in any way compares with that of Shakespeare, this article was also a great source of inspiration and it encouraged us to benefit from the lockdown and make the best use of our spare time to write this book.

Foreword by Robert Sweetow

Tinnitus, the unwanted auditory intruder, is estimated to be experienced by as much as 30 per cent of the world's population and is sufficiently devastating to have a significant negative effect on the daily quality of life for 1–3 per cent of the world's population. Thus, it is abundantly clear that the tinnitus sufferer is not alone. Nevertheless, tinnitus represents a real conundrum for both patients and healthcare professionals. Persons affected by this annoying problem are frequently told by their doctor that 'there is no cure for tinnitus, just ignore it and learn to live with it'. Talk about a statement that is easier said than done! One's reaction to tinnitus becomes a conditioned response that leads to the release of chemical transmitters that can then lead to anxiety and/or depression. Receiving a statement like this from a healthcare worker can induce hopelessness and despair. There is a known correlation between one's emotional state and one's ability to cope with tinnitus, so nothing good can come out of this erroneous prognosis from the professional. I say erroneous because decades of research has shown that most individuals with tinnitus can in fact alter their negative outlook on the condition (and often, on life in general) and can habituate to or largely ignore the tinnitus with the proper training. The challenge for patients and professionals alike is to determine who can deliver proper training and how they can master the art and science of delivering it.

Most of the studies done on various tinnitus treatments have not met the strict standards required for being 'evidence-based'. The one approach that has proven successful is cognitive behavioural therapy (CBT), which has been a remarkably successful method of treating anxiety, mood disorders and chronic pain for several decades. Chronic pain has much in common with tinnitus. Both are invisible and thus difficult for others to empathise with, both are highly subject to environmental factors such as noise, both are highly influenced by the individual's level of tolerance. In addition, the impact of pain, like tinnitus, is not restricted only to the patient. It can have a major effect on family, work colleagues and social relationships. Tinnitus and chronic pain can exert devastating effects on an individual's capacity to sleep, work or concentrate, and can negatively alter hope and dreams of the future. Furthermore, mood disorders and anxiety are commonly experienced by tinnitus patients.

Unfortunately, most healthcare workers are not trained to provide CBT to patients. Most otolaryngologists and audiologists do not have the time or training to provide therapy, and most psychologists and psychiatrists are not familiar enough with peripheral and central auditory function to incorporate it into therapeutic intervention. As a result, tinnitus sufferers often must fend for themselves to discover help.

Given the fact that CBT is considered one of the few evidence-based tinnitus treatments and that relatively few healthcare workers are properly prepared to deliver such treatment, it is only logical that self-help approaches have been advocated.

Drs Aazh and Moore are two of the most respected names in the field of tinnitus management, psychoacoustics, experimental psychology and hearing disorders. Between them, they have published literally hundreds of scientific papers and textbooks and have consulted with or managed thousands of tinnitus patients.

In this book, they have created an easy to read, evidence-based CBT programme for people with tinnitus that is filled with examples, relevant metaphors and real-life case histories of individuals who have conquered tinnitus distress via CBT.

I can honestly say that if I had read this book before practising over forty years of tinnitus management, I would definitely have been a more effective therapist and clinician. In fact, if I were still practising, this book would have become my go-to reference for treating patients and for dealing with my own personal challenges with tinnitus.

Robert W. Sweetow, PhD
Professor Emeritus
Department of Otolaryngology, Head and Neck Surgery
University of California, San Francisco

Who Are We?

Hashir Aazh

I am from Tehran, Iran. I moved to the UK in 2004 and started working as an audiologist in clinics in London and Surrey. I have treated thousands of patients with tinnitus, hyperacusis and misophonia, trained and supervised over a thousand audiologists and psychologists in my tinnitus masterclasses, and published over fifty research papers in the field of audiology. I am Honorary Hearing Research Consultant at the Royal Surrey NHS Foundation Trust (UK), Affiliate Associate Professor at Florida Atlantic University (USA) and Visiting Research Fellow at the University of Surrey (UK). I have served as managing editor of the journal *Noise and Health*, associate editor of the *International Journal of Audiology*, a member of the editorial board of the journal *Auditory and Vestibular Research*, and secretary of the *British Society of Audiology*. I am the organiser of the International Hyperacusis and Misophonia Conference. I have a small private practice, which is dedicated exclusively to supporting adults and children experiencing tinnitus, hyperacusis and misophonia via the use of CBT, in Guildford, London and internationally via video calls.

Brian Moore

I am Emeritus Professor of Auditory Perception in the University of Cambridge. My research interests are: the perception of sound; development of new diagnostic tests of hearing; hearing loss, tinnitus, hyperacusis; and design and fitting of hearing aids. I am a Fellow of the Royal Society, the Academy of Medical Sciences, the Acoustical Society of America, the Audio Engineering Society, the British Society of Audiology and the Association for Psychological Science, and an Honorary Fellow of the Belgian Society of Audiology and the British Society of Hearing Aid Audiologists. I have written or edited twenty-one books and over 730 scientific papers and book chapters. I have been awarded the Littler Prize and the Littler Lecture of the British Society of Audiology, the Silver and Gold medals of the Acoustical Society of America, the first International Award in Hearing from the American Academy of Audiology, the Award of Merit from the Association for Research in Otolaryngology, the Hugh Knowles Prize for Distinguished Achievement, the Life Achievement Award from the American Auditory Society and an honorary doctorate from Adam Mickiewicz University, Poland. I am wine steward of Wolfson College, Cambridge. In my spare time I like playing the guitar and fixing things.

Introduction

If you have this book in your hands, the chances are that you do not need a definition of tinnitus. You know how it feels to hear it, either from your own first-hand experience or from the accounts of those who are affected by it. In this section, we describe some of the common experiences and feelings of people who are distressed by tinnitus and who have not yet embarked on CBT. Your own experiences and feelings may be similar to or more or less severe than those described below. You may find many of the cases described to be very upsetting. But please hang in there! There is light at the end of the tunnel and hope is not lost.

Many of us may believe that it is only natural to experience feelings of anxiety, sadness and irritation if our head is buzzing day and night, non-stop. Even if the tinnitus did stop at times, this would not count as a real relief, because it could come back at any time. We may think of tinnitus as a little beast, sitting on our shoulder, waiting to steal our happiness (as one patient described it), weaken us, make us irascible, a person that we do not want to be and, last but not least, trying to steal our hopes of a satisfying life, of achieving our goals, of being helpful to others and simply of being normal. Perhaps our tinnitus gives us an excuse not to achieve all the things that we have aspired to do. That makes us feel even more disappointed in ourselves.

What effects do people expect tinnitus to have? Perhaps they expect annoyance, and a sense of failure, unfairness and isolation. Many people, even those with no experience of tinnitus, would agree that if they were hearing an unpleasant noise hissing away in their ears, they would not be able to concentrate at work, read, write or make a meaningful contribution to society. Many people would agree that if they were hearing a horrific constant noise, like a demon trapped in their head screaming out loud that it wants to get out, they would go crazy. These were the words of a patient in the psychiatric ward in our hospital who wanted to put a hole in his forehead to let this demon out. With tinnitus, how can we enjoy normal day-to-day activities or get any work done? How can we get enough sleep and remain healthy? Most people would agree that they would not be able to do any of these with an intense experience of tinnitus. For some, this intense pressure can cause aggression. Here is what a patient in our clinic said about tinnitus-induced aggression:

> *It's like being under the worst tension I can possibly be under. As I said to the psychiatrist, if somebody told me to rip your head off, Hashir, to stop this agony, I would consider it, even though we are friends. I like you, but this is not a good place to be. Since half past four in the morning, I have had no sleep, and this has been going on since last Friday. The noise in my head is the worst it can get. Put*

me in a war zone. I will fight everyone in sight, including my own comrades! Please stop it. This is too intense.

This may not be a typical experience of tinnitus, but it clearly demonstrates a state of mind in which horrific actions may be contemplated in order to escape from something unbearable. Such a state of mind can occur when we experience anything that produces overpowering emotions. One example is when we are in love! For example, in Shakespeare's *Romeo and Juliet*, Juliet felt that her life would be meaningless without Romeo. She preferred to be '*chain[ed. . .] with roaring bears*', or to be '*hidden with a dead man in his tomb with rattling bones, reeky shanks and yellow chapless skulls*' over losing Romeo. We may not be able to see how we can live with tinnitus, just as we may be unable to see how we can live without the person that we love.

Figure 1: *Juliet preferred the most terrifying situations over losing Romeo in Shakespeare's* Romeo and Juliet *(1597). As they say: 'love can blind people'. It is not only love that can blind us. Fear does that too. This book aims to teach us how to prevent our fears about tinnitus from blinding us.*

Tinnitus-induced tensions can distort our thinking and make us afraid of what we might end up doing. To make matters worse, very often tinnitus can be perceived as stopping us from hearing external sounds. We may feel that external sounds have to pass through the barrier of tinnitus in order to be heard. We may also feel that tinnitus distorts external sounds and makes it harder for us to communicate with others. One of the patients in our clinic used to tell us that tinnitus was like a fog affecting her hearing. Her words were *'How can an architect build a construction if a thick fog is blurring their vision? This is how tinnitus is affecting me'*.

The terrorising fear of what might happen if tinnitus gets worse often casts a gloomy shadow over all aspects of our life. We may feel obliged to avoid certain activities, foods or environments in the fear that they might make our tinnitus worse. Sometimes the fear of what will happen if tinnitus gets worse limits our life far more than the tinnitus itself. The more we change our life because of tinnitus, the more important the tinnitus becomes. When tinnitus becomes more important to us, it is perceived more strongly, the very outcome that we were trying to avoid. Even seemingly harmless forms of avoidance and rituals like playing music in the background to take our mind off tinnitus and help us to sleep, drinking a special cup of herbal tea to calm us down, listening to noise to take the edge off our tinnitus or searching the Internet for a cure, can make us believe that tinnitus is tolerable only if we behave in a certain way. Perhaps these behaviours can make us feel reassured in the short term that there is something that we can do to gain control over our tinnitus. But we remain fearful about what might happen in the future if these remedies stop working, which is often the case with avoidance behaviours and rituals. There may come a night when no matter how loud the background music is, we still hear tinnitus and cannot get it out of our mind. This increases our feeling of hopelessness, as if our back is against a wall. Certain strategies that we might think are helpful can in fact be counterproductive.

Of course we want to get out of this vicious cycle. Of course we want to be able to lead a normal life despite the tinnitus. Well, this is the second-best option, in the absence of a cure! But often we may feel stuck. We may feel that tinnitus is sapping our motivation, vitality and joy of life. We may feel as if we are stuck in a swamp. We may develop resentment toward ourselves. We may feel disappointed that we have failed to get over these problems. We may feel that we are letting ourselves, our family or friends down. We may feel guilty for letting tinnitus impose a strain on our relationships with our spouses, children, parents, friends and colleagues. All this can snowball into a sense of worthlessness and failure. One patient described her experience like this:

> This clicking tinnitus disturbs my sleep. I am worried that I also disturb my husband's sleep. I will be tired all the time the next day. I will not be able to get anything done, either chores or hobbies or even urgent matters, due to lack of concentration. This makes me feel lazy. I do not get any enjoyment or satisfaction from life. I feel that I am not a nice person. I am good for nothing. That's

> *how tinnitus makes me feel. Being useless makes me feel*
> *devastated, extremely sad and worthless. If I don't play a*
> *part in my family and society, then I am not important,*
> *and it is not worth me being here.*

She was concerned that because of the effect of tinnitus on her she would be judged by others as lazy or not being a good wife or mother. Tinnitus made it hard for her to perform to her own standards and hence created a lot of disappointment and other negative emotions.

Often, we do our best to keep our motivation high and try to distract ourselves from tinnitus as much as we can. This can give us a sense of control and perhaps a sense of normality, because whenever we are fully engaged in an activity, we may not notice our tinnitus. But after a while we may feel exhausted with constantly trying to be fully engaged with a task. Every time that we are not distracted from the tinnitus, we may feel even more disappointed that we are still hearing it and there is no sign of progress. Also, the activities that we use for distraction may not feel natural or enjoyable to us, or even may not properly take our mind off tinnitus. One patient in our clinic described his experience of trying to take his mind off tinnitus as 'kidding' himself. He said:

> *Every time that I do something to take my mind off my*
> *tinnitus, it seems to me that I am kidding myself. For*
> *instance, I went out and bought some paint and crayons*
> *to start painting. Then I thought to myself that every time*
> *that I did this, I was doing it purely to take my mind off*

my tinnitus, but all the time I paint, I am thinking of it. I need something that suddenly emerges as an interest, so it washes it all away and I don't hear it.

He also agreed that it would not be feasible for him to be engaged in interesting spontaneous activities all the time. There would be times when he just wanted to relax or sleep. He said that going to bed was like being beaten where it hurts the most.

The inability to cope with tinnitus and the sense of failure that accompanies it often trigger another nightmare: the fear of isolation and loneliness. We may believe that our loved ones are so disappointed and frustrated with us that they may abandon us. We may even have vivid images of living somewhere in a gloomy painting on the wall, lonely, isolated and sad; a life that seems to be worthless. We are social animals after all, and isolation is detrimental to our well-being. A patient in our clinic described how he felt very small and lonely in the face of tinnitus. He had vivid images of *'being like a hopeless lonely shrimp in the sea which was about to be taken over by deadly waves of a tsunami'* (Figure 2).

Sometimes we may feel that it was our own fault that we developed tinnitus. Perhaps we should have been more careful to protect our ears. We shouldn't have let this happen to us. Or we may feel angry at others if tinnitus somehow developed following their actions (or lack of action), for example, if it was the result of an accident, a medical procedure/treatment or a failure to diagnose and treat the underlying cause. One

Figure 2: *In the face of tinnitus, we may feel like a hopeless shrimp that is about to be taken over by deadly waves of a tsunami. This book aims to equip us with the skills and knowledge required to feel hopeful that we can deal with tinnitus.*

common fear is that tinnitus is a sign of a more dangerous undiagnosed disease. This fear can often persist even after seeing several doctors who state that there is no sinister underlying cause. What if they are wrong? Would it not make sense to learn more about this ourselves? Perhaps we can find some answers. These thoughts can lead us to engage in a crusade of finding out more about tinnitus and the Holy Grail of a tinnitus cure. Such a crusade can drain our resources and time, somehow becoming a ritual in the form of information and reassurance seeking. Similar to avoidance behaviours, rituals may help us to feel better in the short term, but most people agree that they are not a long-term solution.

Tinnitus sometimes sounds like musical tunes or muffled speech. When we have this kind of tinnitus, it can make us believe that we have a mental illness. We may even be afraid of talking to a doctor about it, for the fear of being diagnosed with dementia or psychosis. Some of us may believe that tinnitus is a punishment for our sins. Some may believe that living with tinnitus is like torture and that life is not worthwhile. A girl in her early twenties who attended our clinic was accompanied by a psychiatric nurse. She was an in-patient in the psychiatric ward because she had started to self-harm and was a danger to herself. Her words still stay with all of us in the tinnitus clinic:

> *Give me a medication to make it better. There must be something that I can try. Anything. If something can make it worse, then something can make it better. Just any sort of medication. I think the medications that I am on, Quetiapine and Diazepine and many others that I have taken in the past, have made it worse. So, if these can make it worse, what can make it better? My tinnitus kept increasing and increasing to this point now. There must be something that can make it better. I always try to make sure that there is noise around me. I sleep with my noise generators on to try to mask my tinnitus. I am not living; I am just coping. It just has got worse in the last three months. It has gone up and up and up and up. Even two or three days ago, it went up. I can hear it now. Just a*

Zizizzzzzzzzz. And that's not the worst one. If that was not on, I could hear the woo woo woo woo. I have got about six to seven noises. And the hissing as well. And it is always there. If I am in the car, I hear it over the car. I can hear it all the time. I just want it to stop. There has to be something that you can give me. Some medication that I can try. Because I am trying to kill myself with it. I am sick of it. I don't want to be alive anymore. I just wake up and it is there. It is torturing me every second of the day. I am suffering. I am tired of hearing it. I can't sleep unless I am medicated. I can't go into any room. When I go to any room I just freak out. I can't go to friends' houses because I hate how quiet their rooms are. There must be some new medication that can help me. I must be able to try one. Please!

It was disheartening to hear that anxiety and tinnitus made life so unbearable for this young person with her whole future ahead of her. Perhaps it may cross our minds that anxiety and tinnitus will stop if we die, something that Sigmund Freud talked about in his death principle. He stated that people fantasise about death as a place with no anxiety. On Internet forums, people have even asked if tinnitus can be heard in the afterlife or if they can find eternal silence there. Of course, we can't know the answer to this, but let us resort to the ingenious masterpiece by the Italian poet and philosopher, Dante Alighieri. Dante, in his *Divine Comedy* (1320), did not think that there is silence in the afterlife. He imagined Hell as a place with no music, songs, birds chirping or tweeting, or even the buzzing of bees. But this should not be mistaken for silence. Instead, the sounds that Dante and his guide Virgil encountered going into the *Inferno* were screams, shouts, cries and the unintelligible gurgling and howling of those being punished, which filled the air. So – it would seem to be very unwise to think of death as a way of escaping from tinnitus.

Once a patient in our clinic said that *'the thoughts about tinnitus and its effects on me are actually worse than the tinnitus itself'*. This statement is very revealing; at least part of the problem is not with the tinnitus itself but rather with our thoughts about it. This is not a new idea. The Greek philosopher, Epictetus, in the first century AD wrote in the *Enchiridion*: *'Men are disturbed not by things, but by the views which they take of things.'* So perhaps if we could change our thoughts about tinnitus, our experience of it might also change. We want to be clear that the thoughts that we have about tinnitus should not be considered to be unjustified. There is often some rationale behind these thoughts. Our thoughts are influenced by external events, past experiences, our general health and well-being, and of course our personality. Perhaps learning about the mechanisms by which our thoughts are formed in reaction to tinnitus can help us to get closer to dealing with them in a more constructive way. Our reaction in terms of wanting to get rid of tinnitus, or avoid it if the former is not possible, is quite natural. But could this natural reaction lead to worse outcomes in some circumstances? For example, if we are stuck in quicksand, our instinct might be to try to clamber out. But the more we move and begin to flail our arms and legs, the deeper we sink. So, what our instinct seems to be telling us may not always be helpful. Clambering out may feel like the only solution that we have at the time. Hence, although we may think that avoiding tinnitus with the use of background music or other avoidance techniques is the only solution, these techniques can prevent us from learning how to manage tinnitus without being dependent on them.

Sometimes, we may wish that our tinnitus was softer or had a different quality so that we could better accept it. But that does not seem to be feasible. How can we accept tinnitus as it is? And if we did do that, would it mean that we were simply accepting defeat? Naturally we would prefer to avoid accepting tinnitus. But could this natural reaction be counterproductive? What if we did accept tinnitus as it is? Could such acceptance facilitate a change in our experience of it? In the French fairy tale *Beauty and the Beast* (*La Belle et la Bête*) written by Gabrielle-Suzanne Barbot de Villeneuve (1740), Beauty, the youngest daughter of a merchant, had to live in a palace with a Beast. Every night, the Beast asked her to sleep with him, which Beauty refused to do. She could not understand how it would be possible to love a beast. She was convinced that the Beast had imprisoned the prince of her dreams. Naturally, she wanted to be with the prince of her dreams instead of an ugly beast. After a while, Beauty felt homesick and the Beast allowed her to go back to her family, but on the condition that she returned after exactly one week. When she came back, she found the Beast lying dead in the palace garden. She burst into tears and realised that she could love the Beast. The moment that she fell in love with the Beast, the Beast was transformed into the prince from Beauty's dreams. Could this be the case with tinnitus? Could tinnitus be transformed to something we can cope with if we accept it as it is? Beauty had to accept the Beast as a beast, which naturally was hard and counter-intuitive. But by doing so, the Beast was transformed into a prince. Perhaps the key point is not about accepting our tinnitus. Rather, we need to accept ourselves as who we are, even when our tinnitus is at its worst. By doing so, we may remove barriers from the path of recovery and become the person that we want to be.

However, the experience of tinnitus is far from the stuff of fairy tales. To many of us, tinnitus is an impediment, a disability, a stealer of happiness. How could we feel better by accepting it? We may even feel worse by abandoning our hope that it will go away! What if the solution is not to feel better? Maybe we should feel the agony, anxiety and sadness. Maybe by doing so we would improve our tolerance for the uncomfortable feelings that tinnitus might cause. After all, these emotions are not alien. They are common human emotions. In fact, negative feelings are inevitable during our daily life. There will always be things that make us feel anxious, angry or depressed. If that is the case, and these emotions are unavoidable, then it might make sense to improve our tolerance of them. What benefit might we achieve by simply accepting the negative emotions that tinnitus can cause?

It is true that, ultimately, we aim to defeat tinnitus and mini-mise our negative feelings associated with it. But perhaps we should not rush into rejecting negative emotions out of fear of being unable to cope with them. Think of the 'Rumble in the Jungle', a boxing match with Muhammad Ali fighting the previously undefeated heavyweight champion of the world, George Foreman. Of course, Ali's aim was to deliver a knockout punch to Foreman. But he did not rush in using all his might and throwing his best punches as soon as the match started. First, he took some punches to warm up and measure up his opponent. He got close to him, even whispered in his ear, without fear of being hurt. After all, hurt is an inevitable part of boxing. Often, he leaned on the ropes and went through the pain of Foreman's mighty jabs, uppercuts and hooks, until Foreman weakened and slowed, and Ali found an opportunity to deliver his killer punch in the eighth round, winning the match by a knockout. Annoyance, irritation, sadness and other negative emotions are also part of the match if we want to learn how to beat tinnitus. In boxing, if we throw our best punches as soon as the match starts, in the fear of being hurt, then we may not achieve the best outcome. Fear will blur our vision. We should overcome our fear of the inevitable pain if we are in a boxing match. In boxing, it is not possible to give of our best if we are thinking of avoiding pain. Even if we want to avoid pain, we will still feel it. Perhaps tinnitus management is not possible if we are afraid of having uncomfortable emotions. Perhaps the only way out is through! As the German philosopher Friedrich Nietzsche famously said: 'That which does not kill us makes us stronger.'

There are many factors we need to take into account for the successful management of tinnitus. The treatment should:

- give relief from tinnitus distress

- be lasting

- not be based on false hope

- depend on a change from within the person

- provide the opportunity to flourish and be a more resilient and confident human being

Think of it in this way. If we ranked ourselves as '1' before tinnitus, and tinnitus made us 'minus 1', we should not settle for '0' or even '1'. When we go through the marathon of tinnitus management, we should emerge as '1 plus', a better version of ourselves than we were before the tinnitus!

Maybe the management of tinnitus should be different for each person. After all, we are all different, our circumstances are different, and our tinnitus may be different. This book aims to offer a menu of techniques that we can customise and use should we decide that they can be beneficial to us. But reading this book may not make us feel better. This book is not a relaxing book. It takes us through various stages in the harsh landscape of tinnitus management. There will be several mountains to climb and marathons to run before we fully learn what we need to do. There will be punches that we need to take, pain to tolerate and tiredness to endure. There may be sadness, anger and irritation that we need to feel before happiness, pleasure and delight emerge. So, this is not designed to be an easy ride. As the saying goes, no pain no gain! But the good news is that the materials in this book are carefully put together to fully prepare us for each challenge. We will not be entering the experiments or tasks without choosing to do so nor without having gained enough knowledge and skills to do so. This book is designed to empower us during each stage to move forward, should we choose to do so.

What's inside?

The aim of this book is to give clear directions for getting over tinnitus in ten steps based on CBT. The steps describe the various actions that we need to take, the knowledge that we need to acquire, and the CBT skills that we need to master on the journey of tinnitus management. These ten steps are spread over three overarching parts. There is no set time frame for completing each step or part. The time taken can vary a lot from one person to the next. The important thing is to avoid rushing through the book and the exercises. This is not a quick fix. In our clinics, for most patients a CBT programme for tinnitus management takes between six and fourteen sessions spread over three to twelve months. You should expect to spend a comparable time working through the ten steps in this book. Also, please work through the steps in order; do not try to skip steps or jump to steps that seem more interesting or important. As you work through the steps, you will be asked at various points to fill in tables or worksheets with your own thoughts and experiences. You can do this in the book itself, in a separate notebook or on a computer, or you can download printable versions of these exercises from https://overcoming. co.uk/715/resources-to-download.

Part I is aimed at getting to know tinnitus better and covers the first two steps, which are: Step 1: Learning About Tinnitus, and Step 2: Self-Assessment. Many facts are discussed in Step 1 to help us learn about tinnitus. Although there is a huge amount of information on tinnitus, and many published research studies, it would be impractical and even counterproductive to review all of these in a self-help book. Therefore, the materials presented in Step 1 are carefully picked based on the common questions that tinnitus patients ask, common misconceptions about tinnitus, and the data that can help us to make sense of our experience of tinnitus. But we should not get side-tracked by the endless search for the mechanisms of tinnitus and its possible cures.

Step 2 is about self-assessment with the aim of helping us to evaluate our own experience of tinnitus and its related symptoms and the extent to which these affect us. In this way, we can be more prepared if we decide to seek help from a medical professional and we will have a better idea about the help that we should seek (if needed).

Part II is dedicated to preparing us for CBT. It covers Steps 3 to 5, which are: Step 3: Learn about CBT; Step 4: Test the Water!; and Step 5: Ready for the Real Thing? These three steps form the preparation part of this book and help us to create a sound foundation upon which CBT can be learned and implemented. Before embarking on practising CBT, we need to make sure that what it can offer is what we are after. The application of CBT is not an easy task that can be learned in few days. The techniques of CBT do not come naturally to us. But lots of things are not easy and do not come naturally to us, like playing the piano or swimming. We need to take lessons, learn the theory, and practise playing the piano or swimming properly. The same applies to CBT. In Step 3, we discuss the theoretical underpinnings of CBT and its relevance to the management of tinnitus. Before being able to use CBT, we need to do some preparatory work. We need to learn the principles of CBT and its aims. It is important to learn how CBT is based on a specific way of thinking about tinnitus-related distress. If we can look at tinnitus distress through the lens of CBT, it will become easier to realise how the problems caused by tinnitus can be managed using this method. But to learn these things, we need to go back to the basics and learn CBT theory and the two-way interactions between our thoughts and our emotional and behavioural reactions.

Step 4 is to 'test the water' and try out some of the introductory CBT skills in order to get a sense of how this might work. Only by testing these skills can we decide if CBT is something that we would like to pursue. The introductory skills include tackling avoidance behaviours and rituals, and facing our fears. Our fears will not stay with us forever if we face them. On the other hand, they may stay with us for our entire life if we run away from them! We also need to practise identifying our key troublesome negative thoughts, known as 'hot' thoughts. It is important to build the skill of becoming mindful of our thoughts and evaluating them. This is not a skill that comes naturally to us; hence, we need practice. Finally, it is important to know when to do CBT. This is another important prelimin-ary skill, because it helps us to understand the situations in which CBT can help us and to distinguish them from situations in which it cannot.

Step 5 is the final step in the preparatory part. It helps us to take stock of what we have achieved so far in dealing with tinnitus and to identify room for improvement. Step 5 is the step that will help us decide if we are ready for the real thing! This step presents a quiz that can be used to self-evaluate our confidence in managing tinnitus and how it can be improved. We need to assess how confident we currently are in carrying out our day-to-day tasks, resting and relaxing, and enjoying life even with tinnitus. Also, we need to think how confident we are in doing all these without using any distraction or avoidance. Finally, we need to think about what can help us to become more confident in doing these things. Step 5 helps us to strengthen our motivation and commitment to using CBT to manage our tinnitus. If we conclude that CBT can guide us in the path of recovery and that we are ready to engage in this process, then we can move on to Part III.

Part III is the treatment programme and covers Steps 6 to 10, which are: Step 6: Customise Your Treatment; Step 7: Start to SEL!; Step 8: Let the Sunshine in!; Step 9: Gloves are off! KKIS it!; and Step 10: CBStyle.

Step 6 helps us to customise the treatment by creating a cognitive behavioural model that can explain the mechanism by which we are distressed by our tinnitus, also called the CBT formulation. This customised model can help us to put our experience of tinnitus distress in perspective and analyse the thoughts, emotions and behaviours that negatively affect us. Everyone is different and there is no one way that tinnitus affects people. We can use the template model in Step 6 to describe our tinnitus distress by writing down our own thoughts, emotions, bodily sensations and behaviours in the spaces provided in the template model. This will provide us with the opportunity to think about which parts of the vicious cycle leading to tinnitus distress can be changed or modified. In addition to these, we can use the Tinnitus Reaction Source worksheet to explore various personal and life factors that might have contributed to the reaction that we had to tinnitus in the first place. Why did we develop certain thoughts, emotions, bodily sensations and behaviours as part of our reaction to tinnitus? In this step, we can develop an understanding of the rationale behind our initial reaction to tinnitus, and we can appreciate that it was inevitable given the circumstances that we were in and our personal factors. This will prepare us for embarking on the journey of modifying our thoughts, emotions and behaviours. But not too fast! There is one more step to take before starting the modification phase.

Step 7 builds on the preparation that we did in Step 4 with regard to understanding our avoidance behaviours and rituals. It teaches us to *Stop* our avoidance behaviours and rituals, *Expose* ourselves to tinnitus and to *Learn* from it, a process we call 'SEL' (*Stop-Expose-Learn*) for short. Learning from our behaviour and its consequences, something that happens during SEL, is one of the most powerful strategies for learning. During SEL, we practise controlling our urges to use background noise or any other distractions or rituals when hearing tinnitus, and we expose ourselves to what we are afraid of and learn if we can tolerate the uncomfortable feelings that tinnitus might produce. It is vital that we do not use the main CBT skills (Steps 8 and 9) in an attempt to escape our fear. The only way to become more tolerant of the negative feelings that tinnitus might cause is to experience them. Simply by experiencing anxiety, irritation and sadness, we will improve our tolerance of them. In this way, we will not rush into using the final skills of CBT in the fear of not being able to tolerate the uncomfortable feelings that may be involved. Instead, we will go beyond the fear of experiencing the inevitable human emotions and use CBT skills to stop the vicious cycle of tinnitus distress.

Step 8 helps us to turn our learning from SEL into the antidote for our troublesome thoughts, in other words how the sunshine can remove the darkness. Step 8 involves creating counter-statements that are used to neutralise the effect of negative tinnitus-related thoughts. This is not an easy task since counter-statements need be related to the negative thoughts without having the same errors of judgement (or thought distortions). There are certain criteria that effective counter-statements need to meet. They need to be: relevant and contradictory to the corresponding negative thought; positively worded; and believable to us. It is in this step that we practise blowing away the dark clouds of negative thoughts and letting the sunshine in with our rational counter-statements.

In Step 9, the 'gloves are off' and it is time to put together everything that we practised throughout the previous steps and to break the vicious cycle that leads to distressing tinnitus. Breaking the vicious cycle means that although we hear tinnitus, it does not cause distress. When this happens tinnitus loses its significance, and it is more likely that it will fade away into the background. Step 9 is an ongoing process that we call KKIS (*Know, Keep on, Identify and Substitute*), which we need to use whenever tinnitus bothers us. This involves *Knowing* when to do CBT, which is whenever tinnitus is interrupting our activities or affecting our mood. We also need to *Keep on* dealing with the negative emotions in order to steady the ship. Once steady and unafraid of uncomfortable emotions we will be ready to move on to *Identifying* our negative thoughts about tinnitus and to *Substituting* them with counter-statements. In this step, we will also go deeper and revisit some of our rigid rules of life and basic beliefs about ourselves, life in general, and the future. This can give more depth to our tinnitus management programme.

The final step, Step 10, is about maintaining our progress by preparing ourselves for setbacks. Setbacks are part of normal life and, if we are prepared, it is less likely that they will escalate into a full-blown relapse. The main way of being ready to deal with setbacks is to make sure that our CBT skills are not forgotten. To do this we need to integrate CBT into our lifestyle, an action named *CBStyle*.

The table opposite gives a summary of the ten steps that we need to take to develop proficiency in managing tinnitus. The steps are spread across three overarching parts: Part I: Getting to know tinnitus; Part II: Preparation for treatment; and Part III: Treatment plan.

Part I	Getting to know tinnitus
Step 1: Learn about tinnitus.	One of the main stress-producing effects of tinnitus is fear of the unknown. This step provides us with essential information we need to prepare for the path of recovery.
Step 2: Self-assessment.	This step helps us to be more prepared when seeking help from a medical professional and it can also help us to decide about the type of help that we would like.
Part II	**Preparation for treatment**
Step 3: Learn about CBT.	In this step, we learn about the theoretical underpinnings and principles of CBT.
Step 4: Test the water!	Before fully committing to CBT, we need to 'test the water' and practise some of the introductory skills that are needed in CBT.
Step 5: Ready for the real thing?	This step helps us to strengthen our motivation and commitment to using CBT to manage our tinnitus.

Part III	Treatment plan
Step 6: Customise treatment.	In this step we create a customised model for our tinnitus distress. In addition, we explore various personal and life factors that might have contributed to the reaction that we had to tinnitus in the first place.
Step 7: Start to SEL!	SEL stands for *Stop-Expose-Learn*, a CBT exercise in which we *Stop* our avoidance behaviours and rituals, *Expose* ourselves to tinnitus, and *Learn* from it.
Step 8: Let the sunshine in!	In this step we learn to create counter-statements and practise blowing away the dark clouds of negative thoughts and letting the sunshine in with our rational counter-statements.
Step 9: Gloves are off! KKIS it!	Step 9 is an ongoing process called KKIS, which stands for a CBT exercise (*Know, Keep on, Identify and Substitute*) in which we practise *Knowing* when to do CBT, *Keep on* dealing with the negative emotions, *Identify* irrational thoughts and *Substitute* them with counter-statements.

Step 10: CBStyle.	The final step is to prepare ourselves for setbacks by integrating CBT into our lifestyle, an action named *CBStyle*.

The final chapter is an introduction to the concept of positive psychology for tinnitus management. This is not a usual component of CBT but is very relevant to getting over tinnitus and ensuring a more grounded recovery. Positive psychology helps us to develop acceptance of the experience of tinnitus by putting it in a bigger context. Although it may be difficult to accept tinnitus, this may be much more achievable if you aim to accept 'you' as you are. In the other words, you should accept everything that you have and are, including your tinnitus, instead of trying to accept tinnitus without acknowledging the wider context. So, the question is: 'Am I acceptable to me?' instead of 'Is tinnitus acceptable to me?' The use of positive psychology in combination with CBT for the management of tinnitus is a method that we have been using over the last ten years and are now introducing in this book.

For many people with tinnitus, an ideal treatment would be to get rid of the tinnitus; people often say that they want a pill that cures their tinnitus. The recovery described here does not offer that. It is important to think about the gap between what we want and what can be achieved. Do we want to obtain relief from tinnitus? If so, take a moment to think how your life would be different if in a few months' time you still heard your tinnitus but it had little or no impact on your activities or mood? Imagine that you can still hear your tinnitus, but you are no longer afraid; rather, you feel confident that you can handle it, you are confident that you can enjoy your life and do the things that you like doing, and you are fearless. Would this make any difference to your life compared to now? Please write down your thoughts in the space provided below:

If after reading this book I still hear tinnitus but am not afraid of it anymore, then I will be able to . . .

_____

_____

_____

If after reading this book I feel confident that I can handle tinnitus, then my mood will be different compared to now in the following ways . . .

_____

_____

_____

If after reading this book I feel confident that I can enjoy my life fully even with tinnitus, then my quality of life will improve compared to now in the following ways . . .

_____

_____

_____

PART I

Getting to Know Tinnitus

This part is intended to inform you about some basic aspects of tinnitus and to help you evaluate your own experience of tinnitus.

Step 1. Learn about Tinnitus

When we experience tinnitus for the first time, it is important to see a physician, audiologist or otolaryngologist (ENT doctor) to assess our general health and screen for any disorders of the ear and hearing. These specialists can help to ensure that tinnitus is not a symptom of a medical condition that needs treatment. After medical and audiological evaluations, we can either get 'clearance' that tinnitus is not associated with an underlying disease, or we discover that there may be an underlying medical condition related to tinnitus. An esteemed colleague in Australia, Joey Remenyi, argued in her recently published book, *Rock Steady*, that we need to seek medical clearance rather than a definitive diagnosis, because for most people the exact reason(s) for tinnitus remain unknown and seeking certainty is a wild goose chase. If a medical cause is identified, then the doctor will explore treatment options (if available) for the underlying condition. These treatments often focus on the underlying condition and are not aimed at reducing or eradicating tinnitus, although this sometimes does happen. For a few people, tinnitus disappears with the passage of time but for others it persists regardless of any treatment that they might receive for an underlying condition. For the latter, it is important to learn to manage tinnitus and its effects on our emotions and behaviours.

One of the main stress-producing effects of tinnitus is fear of the unknown. There are lots of research studies demonstrating that education and enhancement of knowledge about tinnitus is a very important step in tinnitus management, regardless of its cause. It is important to know what tinnitus is and what effects it can and cannot have. If we can't get rid of something, then at least it helps to understand it better.

Woody Allen's 1986 comedy/drama *Hannah and Her Sisters* provides a nice illustration of this point. The film was one of Allen's biggest box office hits and it won Oscars in several categories. The character he plays in the film is a hypochondriac who visits his doctor for some slight hearing and balance problems. When the doctor asks if he hears a ringing or buzzing in his ears, Allen's character realises that he does and he immediately wonders if he is going deaf. Once the results of the hearing tests are back, they show a significant loss of sensitivity to high frequency sounds (sounds with high pitches) in his right ear. At first, he thinks that this is not such a big problem; maybe at the opera he won't be able to hear the soprano's highest notes when the singer is on his right-hand side, but that's about it. But then when the doctor suggests sending him to the hospital for further tests, he becomes frightened by the possibility that his tinnitus and hearing loss could be a symptom of something much worse. He starts searching for possible causes and consequences of his symptoms. Since the film pre-dates the Internet, he resorts to calling some other doctors that he knows. One doctor explains that hearing loss can be hereditary or the result of an infection or a loud noise. But Woody's character asks if it could be something worse and the doctor said that it could be a brain tumour!

From that moment in the film, Woody's character keeps checking for the ringing in his ear and attributing any problems that he is experiencing to his tinnitus. He thinks that he hears his tinnitus every time he blinks. He says, 'Am I going blind too?' He cannot take his mind off the buzzing. He cannot sleep at night. He has a lot of negative thoughts about the brain tumour. He is consumed by the internal battle with his own negative thoughts. Sometimes he tries to convince himself that he is just jumping to conclusions and that he will be fine. He tries to reassure himself by remembering that he is in the middle of New York City, surrounded by familiar people and places and with some of the best doctors in the world. He says, 'Nothing is going to happen to you. You cannot just one day vanish. Keep calm. You will be OK! Don't panic!' But the more he tries to get rid of his negative thoughts and reassure himself that he is fine, the more anxious he becomes. He feels very panicky and thinks that he will die as a result of his tinnitus and the underlying brain tumour.

The main problem for Woody's character was not lack of knowledge about what tinnitus is and what effects it can and cannot have. Rather, his main problem was his hypochondria and the anxiety produced by his tinnitus. For some people, anxiety about tinnitus remains even after hospital tests indicate that their tinnitus is not related to any life-threatening condition. Sometimes people feel that they do not have enough understanding about tinnitus even after visiting their doctor. This chapter helps us to learn some key facts about tinnitus. Understanding these can help us to better manage the distress caused by it.

The Woody Allen film also illustrates the fact that our anxieties do not simply disappear if we try to be positive and reassure ourselves that we will be fine. In this book, we will learn the evidence-based CBT methodology that can be used in managing the anxiety that is related to tinnitus.

What is tinnitus?

Tinnitus is defined as the perception of sound(s) in the absence of a physical sound source outside the body or head. Sometimes, tinnitus arises from sound sources in the body or head. This is called 'objective tinnitus'. For example, tinnitus can be related to sound sources such as: (1) blood flow in vessels in the head and neck; (2) contraction of the muscles of the middle ear and soft palate; (3) noise made by the Eustachian tube (the tube that connects the inside of the eardrum to the upper throat) or temporomandibular joint (the joint that connects your lower jaw to your skull); (4) noise generated by specialist receptor cells in the inner ear. These are known as somatosounds or bodily noises and are very rare. An ENT specialist can arrange certain diagnostic tests if they suspect that you have somatosounds. In most cases of tinnitus, no internal or external sound source can be found. Tinnitus of this type is called 'subjective tinnitus' because it cannot be objectively veri-fied by your doctor. The CBT methodology described in this book can be used for subjective or objective tinnitus. From our clinical experience, there is no difference in the effectiveness of the methods described here between objective and subjective tinnitus. Therefore, we do not distinguish them in this book.

> For most people, tinnitus is not a physical sound. It is a perception of sound without an actual external or internal acoustic source. It probably results from abnormal neural activity in the auditory system that the brain interprets as sound.

Persistent tinnitus is diagnosed when it occurs repeatedly in episodes lasting for more than five minutes. Over 50 per cent of people describe their tinnitus as a high-pitched sound. Other descriptions of tinnitus are a buzzing sound, a hissing noise, roaring, a whistle, ringing, a white noise, static, a plane taking off, clicks, crickets, beeps, a humming noise, a heartbeat or a pulsing sound. Some people are unable to describe what their tinnitus sounds like. Tinnitus can be perceived in one ear, both ears or in the centre or back of the head. Some people perceive tinnitus as an outside sound. It is not uncommon that people look for an external sound source at home or in a workplace when they initially notice tinnitus. For example, one person was convinced that there was a wasps' nest above the ceiling in her bedroom.

What causes tinnitus?

For most people, tinnitus is not associated with an underlying disease, with the exception of hearing loss. It seems that tinnitus is nearly always associated with some form of damage to the auditory system, even when that damage is very mild and is not revealed by the standard tests that are done in audiology clinics. If you develop tinnitus, it is very important to see an appropriate medical specialist to investigate the underlying cause. Sometimes tinnitus can be a symptom of certain medical conditions, including: impacted ear wax (also called cerumen), Ménière's disease (which is characterised by fluctuating hearing loss, tinnitus and dizziness), acoustic neuroma (also called vestibular schwannoma; this is a benign tumour that grows near the auditory and vestibular nerves), otosclerosis (a growth of bone within the ear), ear infections (viral and bacterial), cholesteatoma (an abnormal skin growth or skin cyst trapped behind the eardrum, or the bone behind the ear), sudden sensorineural hearing loss or tumours of the arteries and veins in the middle ear. The exact mechanism of tinnitus generation in these conditions is not clear and tinnitus may or may not be directly related to the hearing loss caused by them.

There are certain medical conditions that may lead to tinnitus combined with hearing loss. Examples of these are: impacted earwax, Ménière's disease, vestibular schwannoma, otosclerosis, ear infections, cholesteatoma, and vascular tumours. It is important to see an ENT specialist and audiologist in order to exclude these.

In addition to medical conditions that can cause tinnitus combined with hearing loss, tinnitus is a possible side effect of certain drugs, including antidepressants, antipsychotics, opioids, some antibiotics (e.g. aminoglycosides, macrolides, Vancomycin), anti-inflammatories (e.g. salicylate, also called aspirin), antimalarial drugs (e.g. quinine), loop diuretics used to treat high blood pressure (e.g. ethacrynic acid, furosemide, bumetanide), and anticancer drugs (e.g. cisplatin, oxaliplatin). This does not mean that everyone who takes one of these drugs develops tinnitus. Rather, it means that some people who have taken these drugs have reported tinnitus as a side effect. A side effect is defined as an undesirable effect or illness caused by taking drugs for medical treatment.

Among environmental factors that can cause tinnitus combined with hearing loss are trauma (whiplash or head trauma), intense noise (occupational and recreational noise exceeding safe levels), and chemical substances (primarily organic solvents, e.g. benzene, ethylbenzene, toluene, styrene and kerosene).

> Head trauma, certain medications, noise exposure, and exposure to chemical substances are among the known factors that are associated with triggering or worsening tinnitus.

To sum up, based on current medical knowledge, it is impossible to know with certainty the cause of most cases of tinnitus.

Of course, there are some theories as to how tinnitus might be caused, but these are not proven, especially for subjective tinnitus. So, we can choose to search for an answer to a question that tens of thousands of researchers and medical scientists have not yet discovered, or we can choose to stop the search and use our resources to manage our tinnitus. Managing tinnitus is a tall order. It can't be taken lightly, and it needs our full commitment and focus. Based on our clinical experience, regardless of what might have caused your tinnitus in the first place, the CBT methods described in this book can help to manage it. For more in-depth medical information, please read *Tinnitus: A Multidisciplinary Approach* by Professor David Baguley and colleagues (see Further reading).

What are the side effects of tinnitus?

Am I going deaf?

Tinnitus does not appear to hamper our ability to detect and discriminate external sounds, even when the sounds are similar to the tinnitus. However, people often blame tinnitus for their hearing difficulties (if they have them). People hardly ever complain about the impact of tinnitus on their hearing if they do not have any underlying hearing loss. Therefore, in such circumstances, it is likely that the difficulties in hearing are caused primarily by the hearing loss itself, not by the tinnitus. This means that if a person with tinnitus experiences difficulties in hearing conversations, they would probably experience the same sort of hearing difficulties even if they did not have tinnitus. Blaming tinnitus for hearing problems can lead to the development of further irritation with tinnitus, which makes it more noticeable. When you see an audiologist, they will advise you if you have any hearing loss and if hearing aids can improve your hearing.

> Tinnitus probably does not markedly affect our ability to hear. However, tinnitus is nearly always associated with some form of damage to the auditory system.

Sometimes people with tinnitus complain that although sounds are clearly audible, some seem distorted. This is especially the case for musicians. We have seen many classical, pop or rock professional musicians who felt that certain tones sounded distorted to them since they had developed tinnitus. Understandably, the prospect of this affecting their ability to perform in a concert or to edit a recording created a lot of anxiety for them. Perceived distortion of sounds can also occur in noisy environments, such as pubs and restaurants. Distorted hearing can occur in relation to external sounds and/or the person's own voice. It can get worse if the tinnitus becomes louder, or the tinnitus can become louder when the person experiences distorted hearing. However, for some people distorted hearing can be independent from tinnitus. For people whose distorted hearing appears to be linked to their tinnitus, the CBT methods described in this book may reduce the distortion of hearing as well as reducing the distress caused by the tinnitus.

If your hearing test shows normal hearing sensitivity (called in the clinic a normal audiogram) but you have difficulty in discriminating sounds in noisy environments, you confuse similar-sounding words, you struggle to understand rapid speech, you frequently ask for repetition, and/or you have difficulty hearing on the telephone, the problem may be related to an auditory processing disorder (APD). APD is defined as difficulty in the perception of speech and non-speech sounds without any marked hearing loss as measured by the audiogram. APD often co-exists with speech and language problems, dyslexia (difficulty in reading, writing or spelling) and memory or attention disorders. It may be the case that, for some people, APD co-exists with tinnitus. APD can be helped with interventions that improve the listening environment (e.g. reducing reverberation and unnecessary noise) as well as by improving listening skills, technological assistive devices and auditory training. See the APD Guide developed by Professor Nicci Campbell and her colleagues available at www.meshguides.org /guides/node/1432

To sum up, it is recommended that you ask for an APD assessment if you have normal hearing sensitivity but you have to ask people to repeat themselves multiple times per day, struggle to hear on the telephone or struggle more than those around you when trying to understand speech in the presence of background noise.

> Ask for an APD assessment if your hearing sensitivity is within the normal range but you struggle to distinguish words, especially in noisy environments.

Can tinnitus cause headaches or other problems?

Based on clinical observations, there seem to be several sensations that can be related to or caused by tinnitus distress. They range from various forms of muscle tension to oversensitivity to sound, referred to as hyperacusis.

Tension in the head and face muscles can lead to headaches. A study conducted in Sweden by Dr Lugo and colleagues showed that the prevalence of headaches among people with tinnitus was 26 per cent, and up to 40 per cent for people with severe tinnitus. This is higher than the prevalence in the general population. The headaches may be related to the stress and anxiety caused by tinnitus, or they may be related to a pre-existing problem like migraines. If the former is the case, the CBT methods described here may reduce the incidence and/or severity of headaches. If the latter, a doctor may be able to diagnose the root cause of the headaches or prescribe medication for the migraines.

There are tiny muscles attached to the ossicles, the tiny bones in the middle ear that connect the eardrum to the cochlea (part of the inner ear), as illustrated in Figure 3. If the muscles contract, they stiffen the ossicular chain, leading to a reduction in the transmission of sound from the eardrum to the cochlea. This occurs as a natural reflex when we are exposed to an intense sound; it helps to protect the delicate structures inside the cochlea. The muscles relax when the intense sounds stop. However, sometimes the muscles can contract for a long time without any intense sound being present. This can lead to a

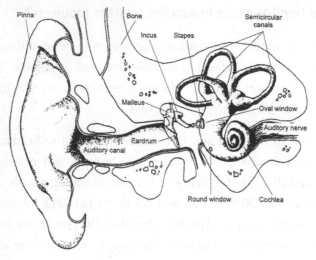

Figure 3: *Schematic diagram of the early stages of the auditory system. Sound travels down the auditory canal causing the eardrum to vibrate. These vibrations are transmitted to the cochlea via three tiny bones, the malleus, incus and stapes, which are collectively called the ossicles. Taken from Moore (2012) An Introduction to the Psychology of Hearing, 6th Edn, Brill, The Netherlands, by permission of the author.*

sense of aural fullness and perception of hearing difficulties. Often the muscles relax during therapy for tinnitus, and such aural fullness disappears. Aural fullness can also occur with ear disorders that affect the cochlea (e.g. Ménière's disease), middle ear (e.g. otitis media and infection of the middle ear) or hearing loss. These will usually be detected when you see an ENT specialist prior to any therapy.

> Sensations related to tinnitus (e.g. aural fullness, headaches and hyperacusis) often improve after tinnitus distress is reduced with the use of CBT.

Why does tinnitus make my ears more sensitive to noise?

Tinnitus distress can be associated with oversensitivity to sound (hyperacusis); sounds that would not bother most people are experienced as unpleasant. The underlying mechanism for this is not clear. However, fear of worsening of tinnitus due to noise exposure is thought to be one contributing factor. The individual may feel (perhaps unconsciously) that they need to prevent their tinnitus from getting worse by avoiding certain sounds in the environment. This condition is also known as tinnitus-induced hyperacusis, and it is more common in people with what is called 'reactive tinnitus'. This term is used to describe tinnitus whose loudness or pitch changes in response to external sounds. Reactive tinnitus is more common among musicians than among non-musicians, but it is not limited to musicians. To minimise the risk of worsening of their tinnitus, a person with reactive tinnitus may constantly aim to control or avoid sounds that influence their tinnitus, or to protect their ears using earmuffs or earplugs. Avoidance behaviour and excessive use of ear protection may contribute to the development and worsening of hyperacusis. Hyperacusis in turn can make it difficult for the individual to understand speech in noisy environments, since the noise can cause discomfort and distract them from the conversation. If the hyperacusis can be managed well via CBT, the resultant difficulties in understanding speech in noisy environments often disappear. Hyperacusis can also be independent of tinnitus.

> Both hyperacusis and tinnitus could be related to how our brain responds to damage to the auditory system. How our brain responds depends partly on cognitive and emotional factors. CBT can help to modify the way that our brain responds to damage to the auditory system.

Will tinnitus drive me mad?

Symptoms of anxiety and depression are common among individuals with tinnitus. However, not everyone with tinnitus who exhibits such symptoms is diagnosed with anxiety or mood disorders when undergoing formal psychological evaluations. It is understandable that tinnitus might make us feel anxious or experience a low mood. We may think that we will not be able to carry out our day-to-day tasks. We may fear that tinnitus will impair our sleep, relationships, general health and quality of life. All these fears can lead to the development of symptoms of anxiety and depression, which in turn increase the impact of tinnitus on our life and make it even harder to cope with tinnitus. A history of mental illness in a person or their parents increases the likelihood of that person feeling anxious or depressed should they develop tinnitus. Based on our research studies that were published in the *American Journal of Audiology* (2018, 2019, 2020), for individuals who suffer from tinnitus, depressive symptoms may be alleviated if tinnitus-induced anxiety, the effect of tinnitus on life and hyperacusis are managed adequately with the use of CBT, even if the loudness of the tinnitus remains unchanged.

Seek help from mental health professionals if you feel that you are experiencing low mood or anxiety. If in your childhood your parents suffered from anxiety, depression, anger, or other psychological disorders, you may be at higher risk of being affected by these if you get tinnitus. Make sure that you seek help if this applies to you.

Having symptoms of depression can increase the risk of developing thoughts that life with tinnitus is meaningless and we are better off dead. This highlights the need to be open about our mental health, especially when dealing with distress-producing conditions like tinnitus. The best course of action when it comes to problems with our mental health is to seek advice from a psychologist or psychiatrist. Being open about our mental health is critical for all of us in any walk of life. In 2019, the Duke and Duchess of Cambridge and Prince Harry supported the 'Heads Together' campaign with the aim of encouraging people to talk to one another openly about their mental health struggles. They emphasised the fact that unresolved mental health problems often prevent us from coping with life challenges. To read more about Heads Together, visit www.headstogether.org.uk

Can I still sleep if I hear tinnitus?

Tinnitus is often associated with difficulties in getting to sleep, staying asleep, going back to sleep if woken up in the middle of the night, and achieving restorative sleep. About 70 per cent of patients seeking help for tinnitus report some form of sleep difficulty. But it is not clear whether the degree of sleep difficulty is related to the loudness or quality of the tinnitus or whether it is related to the psychological impact of the tinnitus.

In a study conducted in our clinic in collaboration with the Universities of Nottingham and Cambridge, we assessed whether the loudness of tinnitus was related to sleep disturbances (insomnia), based on data for 417 patients. The analysis showed that the loudness of tinnitus is only indirectly related to the severity of insomnia. In other words, louder tinnitus does not necessarily lead to more sleep disturbances. The severity of insomnia depends on the amount of depression and annoyance caused by the tinnitus. The more depressed and annoyed a person becomes due to their tinnitus, the more sleep disturbances they tend to experience. According to the theory behind CBT, emotional disturbances such as feeling irritated or depressed are not directly due to hearing tinnitus, but rather are the result of our thoughts about tinnitus and its impact on our behaviours. Therefore, in order to reduce tinnitus-related sleep disturbances, we need to manage our thoughts and behaviours. This is the aim of CBT for tinnitus as described in this book. Listening to music or background noise at night-time is an avoidance behaviour, and it does not address the key cause of the sleep disturbances, namely the tinnitus-related negative thoughts. In the chapters on treatment, we discuss how to use CBT to manage tinnitus-induced sleep difficulties.

Tinnitus may lead to sleep difficulties but these are not directly related to the loudness of the tinnitus. If tinnitus annoyance and depressive symptoms are managed with the use of CBT, then improvements in sleep quality usually follow, regardless of the loudness of tinnitus.

Can I concentrate on my work if I hear tinnitus?

It is not uncommon for people to complain about tinnitus affecting their concentration, either at work or during leisure activities. This can happen even with simple tasks. For example, some people report that because of their tinnitus they cannot follow conversations. As discussed earlier, this is more likely to be a result of an underlying hearing loss than of tinnitus. However, very often people complain that tinnitus affects their concentration when they are working at their computer, reading or even doing a crossword puzzle. So, what is the mechanism by which tinnitus can lead to a lack of concentration? This is important, as it can help us to develop a plan to tackle it.

In 2020, Dr Clarke and colleagues at the University of Nottingham reviewed thirty-eight studies that assessed the association between tinnitus and various cognitive (mental) processes. Their results showed that speed of thinking, short-term memory, long-term memory and the ability to plan and perform complex tasks on average were all poorer for patients with tinnitus than for control groups without tinnitus. However, the authors concluded that the quality of the available research evidence did not allow for a firm conclusion as to whether tinnitus directly contributed to any of these poorer outcomes. For example, symptoms of anxiety and depression are prevalent among patients with tinnitus. Anxiety and depression are known risk factors influencing concentration and thought processes (e.g. if we are depressed, this adversely affects our memory and speed of processing information, and if we are anxious, we tend to make more errors). Since this review was carried out, several groups of researchers have reported results consistent with the idea that tinnitus has no impact on concentration and memory skills. In 2021, Dr Waechter and colleagues at Lund University, Sweden, compared measures of memory and concentration for people with and without tinnitus, matching the groups for age, sex, hearing sensitivity, anxiety and depression. Their results showed that the presence of tinnitus did not imply poorer short-term memory or concentration.

To sum up, although it is understandable to think that tinnitus affects concentration, research evidence does not support this idea. It is more likely that concentration difficulties are primarily caused by the distress produced by tinnitus and perhaps by an underlying hearing loss (if the problem is concentrating on conversations). The good news is that the distress caused by tinnitus can be significantly reduced by the CBT methods described in this book. Hearing difficulties can be alleviated using hearing aids.

CBT and hearing aids (in the case of tinnitus combined with hearing loss) can reduce the concentration difficulties experienced by people who have tinnitus.

What is it like to have tinnitus?

How can our reactions to tinnitus prevent us from recovering from tinnitus distress and how can CBT help us to live well with it? We need to gain a better understanding of the factors that can lead to an escalation of the problem. We need to explore if there is a pattern of misunderstandings and behaviours among those people who are most affected by tinnitus, so that we can learn to avoid these behaviours. After all, we collectively learn from our mistakes. We have built our knowledge base as a species by learning from our mistakes and those of others throughout the centuries. And we keep learning!

Although the experience of tinnitus and its impact on us can vary from person to person, there are some common patterns in our experiences. This self-help guide provides an opportunity for us to develop the skills required to identify these patterns and address them in order to get over tinnitus. In this section, we describe what it is like to have tinnitus for three people: John, Aisha and Felicity. After each person has described their experiences, your task is to complete a table identifying the pattern of unhelpful perceptions and behaviours for that person. You also need to ask yourself this question: if you were going to give them advice, what would it be? After you have completed the tables for all three people, we will discuss the common patterns in their experience of tinnitus.

John: I'm going to have to deal with tinnitus for the rest of my life

John developed tinnitus at the age of fifty-one. He did not have any significant hearing impairment. He felt anxiety and a feeling of blockage in his ears whenever his tinnitus was loud. He was unable to distract himself from his tinnitus. He was worried that he would have to put up with it for ever, which cast a dark shadow over all aspects of his life, making it difficult for him to see the positive side of things. He thought that if his tinnitus got worse, he would not be able to cope, and that life would become worthless. He interpreted his tinnitus as a sign of ill health and did whatever he could to reduce or stop it. For example, he stopped eating chocolate and drinking tea and coffee, even though there is no evidence that chocolate or tea and coffee have an influence on tinnitus, and he constantly tried to distract himself from his tinnitus by avoiding being in a quiet room and by keeping himself busy as much as he could. He also developed some bedtime rituals, such as doing deep breathing exercises and listening to a podcast every night to help him fall asleep. His avoidance behaviours and rituals added a further burden to his life, making him feel dependent on them and worried about what would happen if they lost their effect. He also feared that his tinnitus would get louder and that he would no longer be able to distract himself from it. Constantly trying to reduce his tinnitus or to distract himself from it led him to feel tired and unable to enjoy his life, reinforcing his negative belief that tinnitus would continue to make his life miserable.

His fear of the future put a lot of pressure on him and prevented him from enjoying any activities, even when his tinnitus was not bothersome at that moment. He blamed himself for being affected by his tinnitus and being unable to cope better. He felt that he was inadequate. This perception of being inadequate resonated with his childhood experiences of growing up in an environment where he was never praised by his parents. All these things made him feel more disappointed with himself, making it more difficult for him to cope with his tinnitus.

> Our avoidance behaviours and rituals add a further burden to our life, making us feel dependent on them and afraid of the day that they may not work.

Now complete the worksheet overleaf. We have given some examples for each question, but please do your best to write down John's tinnitus-related thoughts, possible misunderstandings in his thoughts and behaviours, and your advice as to what could help him to get over his tinnitus by changing those thoughts and behaviours. In other words, how could he think or what could he do differently that might help?

John	
List the bothersome thoughts that John had about his tinnitus.	Example 'I will have to put up with this for the rest of my life'
1. _____ 2. _____ 3. _____ 4. _____	
Can you identify any errors of judgement in his thoughts?	Example: Blaming himself for not being able to cope with his tinnitus
1. _____ 2. _____ 3. _____ 4. _____	
What were his behaviours in response to his tinnitus?	Example: He stopped drinking coffee
1. _____ 2. _____	

3. _____

4. _____

What is your advice for John? What changes in his thoughts and behaviours do you think could help him to cope better with his tinnitus?	Example of advice with regard to changing his thoughts: *He should not blame himself. He is only human.*
	Example of advice with regard to changing his behaviours: *There is no need to reduce his caffeine intake as it has nothing to do with tinnitus. Enjoy your coffee!*

1. _____

2. _____

3. _____

4. _____

Aisha: To cope I need to be positive and push away my negative emotions related to tinnitus

Aisha had tinnitus for many years, but it was very mild and did not bother her at all until recently. After a stressful period at work, her tinnitus suddenly got worse. Her tinnitus was constant and heard only in one ear. No underlying medical condition apart from a mild hearing loss was diagnosed following medical examination. Her tinnitus was accompanied by oversensitivity to sounds. Whenever she heard certain sounds, they caused discomfort, leading to fear of her tinnitus getting worse. The sounds that caused discomfort were typical day-to-day environmental noises that were perfectly tolerable to other people, for example announcements in trains and supermarkets, noise in shopping malls, the sound of kitchen appliances, clanking cutlery and water running from the tap. She believed that every time that she was exposed to a loud sound, like somebody clapping their hands, her tinnitus got louder. She felt that this effect might build up over time, leading to her tinnitus getting louder year after year. She believed that she was vulnerable and weak.

Aisha made lots of changes to her life to minimise the risk of her tinnitus getting worse. For example, she did not accept a promotion at work for fear of the additional stress that it might bring. She thought that managing stress would help to reduce her tinnitus. Yet her tinnitus continued despite her attempts to reduce stress. This made her more disappointed and she felt that she was failing. She also avoided a wide range of social situations and activities that might be noisy and might increase her tinnitus.

The more her decisions were driven by her fear of her tinnitus getting worse, the more important her tinnitus became, making her even more aware of it. She believed that in order to cope she should push away the negative emotions caused by tinnitus and focus on positive things. However, the more she tried to push away her tinnitus-related negative emotions, the more they pushed back. This was very draining for her, and she described it as being trapped in a mental battle.

> Trying to push back the uncomfortable emotions caused by tinnitus is like trying to push away a cloud of sticky slime. Our hands will surely get stuck.

Now complete the worksheet overleaf for Aisha.

Aisha	
List the bothersome thoughts that Aisha had about her tinnitus.	Example: I am vulnerable and weak
1. _____ 2. _____ 3. _____ 4. _____	
Can you identify any errors of judgement in her thoughts?	Example: Labelling herself as weak.
1. _____ 2. _____ 3. _____ 4. _____	
What were her behaviours in response to her tinnitus?	Example: She avoided certain activities.
1. _____ 2. _____	

3. _____

4. _____

What is your advice for Aisha? What changes in her thoughts and behaviour do you think could help her to cope better with tinnitus?	Example for her thoughts: She should not label herself as weak. We all have strengths and weaknesses.
	Example for her behaviours: There is no need to avoid certain activities. Tinnitus can go up and down even if you do nothing. Live your life without fear of tinnitus!

1. _____

2. _____

3. _____

4. _____

Felicity: Tinnitus is out of my control!

Felicity developed tinnitus after attending a rock concert in London. She blamed herself for not being more careful and believed that it was her own fault. She was convinced that the concert caused physical damage to her ears which in turn caused the tinnitus. However, all her audiological tests and medical examinations showed nothing abnormal. She believed that nothing could help her unless the physical damage to her ears was repaired. In the absence of a cure, she felt disappointed but especially scared. She felt that she was on her own and that nobody could understand her. Fear of loneliness and isolation increased her anxiety, leading to sleep difficulties, low confidence at work and low mood. She resorted to engaging with Internet forums for people suffering from tinnitus and kept looking for a cure. Although forums and searching the Internet did not help her to manage her tinnitus better, she felt that at least she was doing something about it. This became a ritual for her.

She did not believe that doing CBT and changing her thoughts or behaviours would help at all while her tinnitus was still present. In fact, she was against rehabilitative therapies and thought that these were a waste of time and simply delaying the path of science in finding a cure for tinnitus. Because of her tinnitus, she felt that she could not concentrate on her work. She thought that she could not be as efficient as she used to be. She was worried that it would take her longer to complete work-related tasks and that the quality of her work would be poor due to loss of creativity, which she also thought to be a result of her tinnitus. In the fear of these problems, she avoided going to work and asked to be signed off sick. Her job was in a very competitive (and male-dominated) environment. She was worried that her colleagues would think that she was not performing well at work. She was convinced that she would lose her job if she could not get rid of her tinnitus.

> In our opinion, learning to manage tinnitus by using CBT will not delay the path of science in finding a cure for tinnitus. It will help us to lead a satisfying life, sleep well, improve our mental health and put tinnitus behind us so that we can have some spare capacity to help with the science in any way that we choose.

Now complete the worksheet for Felicity.

Felicity	
List the bothersome thoughts that Felicity had about her tinnitus.	Example: My colleagues will think that I am not performing well at work
1. _____ 2. _____ 3. _____ 4. _____	
Can you identify any errors of judgement in her thoughts?	Example: She cannot know what her colleagues think about her unless she can read their minds!
1. _____ 2. _____ 3. _____ 4. _____	
What were her behaviours in response to her tinnitus?	Example: Avoiding work.
1. _____ 2. _____	

3. _____

4. _____

| What is your advice for Felicity? What changes in her thoughts and behaviours do you think could help her to cope better with her tinnitus? | Example for her thoughts: It is impossible to know what others think of us. Therefore, it is better to avoid negative predictions about what they might think. |
| | Example for her behaviours: Avoiding work will prevent you from learning how to manage your tinnitus at work. You may forget about tinnitus when you are at work! |

1. _____

2. _____

3. _____

4. _____

Although each person's experience is unique, we can see that they all adopted certain avoidance and ritualistic behaviours. Such behaviours made them believe that they could not cope if their tinnitus got worse or if they did not perform certain rituals. All these things made their lives more difficult and reduced their joy in life, contributing to their general disappointment and depressed mood. Avoidance prevented them from learning that at least some of their negative predictions were untrue. John's avoidance behaviours were constantly trying to distract himself from tinnitus by avoiding being in a quiet room and keeping himself busy and listening to a podcast every night to help him fall asleep. His rituals were stopping eating chocolate and drinking tea and coffee and doing deep breathing exercises at night. Aisha's avoidance behaviours were not accepting a promotion at work and avoiding a wide range of social situations and activities that might worsen her tinnitus. Felicity's main rituals were engaging in Internet forums for people suffering from tinnitus and constantly looking for a cure. Her avoidance behaviours were avoiding going to work and asking to be signed off sick.

Tinnitus and its associated sensations (e.g. ear fullness and hypersensitivity to sound) can trigger negative thoughts that can lead us to feel difficult and distressing emotions. These sensations, thoughts and feelings can lead us to change our behaviours. Often, we try to change our behaviour in ways that we think might protect us from having these unwanted experiences again. For example, we may listen to background music to distract ourselves from tinnitus while at work or when going to bed at night. Although listening to background music sporadically may help in reducing tinnitus annoyance and its effect on us in the short term, such avoidance behaviour can backfire in the long run. This is because tinnitus is a condition that is usually with us all the time, at work or at rest, and it is generated inside our own head. It is not an outside problem or an external issue to be avoided or masked. When we try to control tinnitus and do things to make it go away, we can develop a belief that this is the only way to cope and that we will not be able to manage if we do not always do this.

This belief may lead us to expend a lot of energy trying to avoid tinnitus and prevent us from learning what would actually happen if we did not distract ourselves from our tinnitus. Maybe we can concentrate at work and fall asleep at night even when hearing tinnitus. In addition, the thought that we must always use some distraction may make us fear a time when we will not be able to distract ourselves from tinnitus for some reason. What if the tinnitus becomes louder and the background music does not work anymore? What if we find ourselves in a situation where it would be impossible to use background music? Over time, avoidance behaviours can intensify and can dominate our lives. Some people end up becoming isolated and abandoning a wide range of activities (e.g. work, socialising, workouts at the gym, listening to or playing music) in the fear that such activities might worsen their tinnitus.

The three people described above, John, Aisha and Felicity, also shared a pattern of negative thoughts about tinnitus and its impact on their health, occupation and general quality of life. All three had thoughts that involved negative predictions of the future. It is erroneous to think that we can predict the future with any accuracy. Most of the time, we cannot be sure what will happen in the future, especially when it comes to thoughts, feelings and behaviours. Thinking negatively about how tinnitus will affect us tends to make us more anxious. The more anxious we get, the less are we able to cope. Anxiety disrupts our sleep and concentration, and we might take this as proof that our negative predictions of the future are correct: a self-fulfilling prophecy.

Examples of predictions of the future were: *I will have to put up with this for the rest of my life*; *If my tinnitus gets worse, I will not be able to cope*; *Every time I am exposed to a loud sound my tinnitus will increase*; *My tinnitus will get louder year after year*; *Nothing can help unless the physical damage is repaired*; *Changing my thoughts and behaviours will not help*; *I will not be able to complete my tasks*; and *My colleagues will think that I am not performing well*.

In addition to predictions of the future, some of John, Aisha and Felicity's thoughts represent all-or-nothing thinking and magnification of the problem: they behaved as if a worst-case scenario were really happening. Examples of this kind of thinking are: *I will be isolated and lonely*; *Life will become worthless*; *I cannot concentrate at work*; *I am no longer efficient*; and *I will lose my job*.

There were also some thoughts that, although they seemed harmless, caused a lot of emotional disturbance, suggesting that they were in conflict with some other rigid underlying beliefs. For example, John thought that *Tinnitus is a sign of ill health*. This bothered him a lot. But why? Most people have some illnesses or poor health at some point during their lives, but they do not spend a lot of time worrying about it. So why did this thought bother John so much? During his therapy sessions it became apparent that he held a rigid belief that *To be happy I must always be normal and I mustn't be ill*. This belief was unrealistic because everyone gets ill at some point in their lives; it is a normal part of life. Moreover, there are many people who have some illnesses but who lead a happy and fulfilling life. If having an illness always led to unhappiness, then most people would be unhappy most of the time. After John recognised that his belief was irrational, he modified it to a more balanced thought that *Illnesses are a normal part of life and happiness can be achieved regardless*.

Before starting therapy, John also had a thought blaming himself: *I am not coping well*. This thought conflicted with a rigid underlying belief that *I must always be strong and resilient*. This belief is unrealistic because we cannot always be strong, efficient and resilient. During the therapy sessions he modified this belief to *I have strength and weaknesses, which is true of any human being*. Changing these rigid underlying beliefs helped him to accept the thoughts that tinnitus is an illness and that he has not coped well with it. Acceptance helped him to cope with his situation and stopped him from blaming himself for not being able to cope with it better.

But what was the root cause of John's rigid beliefs? He could link these to his childhood experiences, which made him develop a core belief that he was inadequate. For example, he recalled that whatever he did was not good enough and he was never praised by his father. He also had vivid memories of rivalry with his siblings, fighting for his dad's attention. He remembered being called a freak by his siblings. His rigid rules of *I must always be strong and resilient* and *To be happy I must always be normal, and I mustn't be ill* seemed to reflect his core belief that *I am inadequate*. In some ways, these rigid rules helped him to avoid situations where the negative core belief might be shown to be true.

During the therapy, John was asked to consider if he was in fact inadequate. On reflection, he realised that he had achieved many things throughout his life. This was the opposite of being inadequate. Although he might have felt inadequate during his childhood, this was no longer relevant to his experience as an adult. Following the therapy, he developed a new core belief that *I am good enough*. He came up with a long list of his personal qualities, character strengths and virtues as well as life and work achievements to support this new core belief.

Aisha thought that *In order to cope, I must be positive and I mustn't feel sad*. On the surface, it may seem logical to think in this way. However, this thought is irrational because sadness is a common human emotion. Sometimes it is appropriate to be sad and the emotion cannot be artificially dampened down or eliminated. You can probably think of many circumstances where it would be inappropriate not to feel sad; for example, when you hear of the death of a friend or family member. In Aisha's case, whenever she felt upset or annoyed by her tinnitus, she also felt that she was failing to remain positive, which made her even more upset. During her therapy, Aisha modified this thought to *I have a wide range of emotions from happiness to sadness and all of these have a purpose. Therefore, it is OK to feel them*. This new thought removed the pressure, or the mental battle as she described it, to push the sadness away.

The need to push away negative feelings came from her negative core belief that *I am vulnerable and weak*. Her core belief was developed based on some of her childhood experiences of feeling weak and vulnerable when her mother was mentally ill and had to be hospitalised for several months. These events made her feel very vulnerable throughout her childhood. She believed that due to her weakness and vulnerability she would not be able to survive. As a result, during her childhood, she developed the rule *In order to cope, I must be positive and I mustn't feel sad*. Although she might have felt vulnerable and weak due to certain circumstances in her childhood, this was not the case for her as an adult. Moreover, vulnerability and weakness are part of human experience. We all have weaknesses and vulnerabilities. During her therapy, Aisha developed a much more balanced core belief that *I have strengths and weaknesses*. This created a fundamental change in her attitude toward her thoughts about tinnitus and the emotions induced by them.

Felicity blamed herself for not being careful enough in protecting her ears. She often thought *It's my own fault*. This thought carried a huge emotional burden. But why couldn't she just accept the fact that things like this happen, without any fault on her part? When she went to the rock concert, she did not know that she would get tinnitus and that her tinnitus would be severe. Many people do not use ear protection when they go to rock concerts. We all do things that in one way or another can harm ourselves or people around us. That's just our nature. For example, many of our behaviours harm our environment and our own health. Some of them have been recognised through accumulated human knowledge over time, but there is no doubt that there are many things we do now that seem innocuous but will be deemed as harmful in the future. We can learn from our mistakes but, also, we should be able to forgive and forget. The fact that Felicity felt a significant negative emotional burden of her thought that *It's my own fault* indicates a possible conflict with some of her rigid beliefs and rules of life.

Just as for Aisha and John, Felicity had some rigid rules for living. For example, one of her rules was *I should be able to find a quick solution to every problem*. She felt that she was a failure if she was unable to solve her problems. During her therapy she asked herself *What does it mean to me if I fail?* This helped her to realise that in her mind being a failure would result in people abandoning her, leading to loneliness and isolation. Another rule was *I should never hurt anybody else*. She asked herself *What is the worst that I can imagine happening if I hurt others?* This helped her to realise that, just as for her thoughts on failure, in her mind hurting others would result in people abandoning her, again leading to loneliness and isolation. During her therapy sessions she challenged these rules and came up with more balanced thoughts, for example: *I can do my best. Sometimes I will be able to solve problems. But there are problems whose solution is beyond me or beyond the current state of knowledge* and *It is inevitable that people around me will get hurt due to something that I do or say at some point during my life. Most of the time they will get over it* and *I live in a society and there is always someone to talk to.*

So far, we have discovered that fear of isolation and loneliness were important parts of Felicity's thoughts. Of course, we are social animals, and isolation and loneliness are generally feared and disliked. But was this the root cause of her negative emotions? As a person, she was very conscious of always having to do the right thing and be a good person. She felt that in order to be a good person she should please people around her. Some of her childhood experiences, including a poor relationship with her parents and strict religious teaching from her grandmother, planted the belief in her mind that she was not a good person and that to be good she must not be herself. These beliefs might not have been what her grandmother was trying to teach her, but they were her interpretation of what she was told. She believed that she must be the person that other people wanted her to be and only in that way would people want to be with her.

Her therapy helped her to think about the meaning behind her loneliness and isolation. She discovered that deep down she felt that *I am unworthy*. She could recall some of her childhood memories of feeling unworthy, due either to conflicts with her parents or to her grandmother's strict religious ideas or at least to her interpretation of them at such a young age. During the final stages of her therapy, she learned to put 'worthiness' on a continuum and to think of the characteristics of a person who is very worthy and a person who is very unworthy, at the extreme ends of the continuum. Next, she had to think where she was on the continuum. In fact, she rated herself as very close to a moderately worthy person. This helped her to challenge her core belief that *I am unworthy* and change it to *I am worthy*. This, together with changing her irrational rules, as described earlier, helped her to have a more accepting attitude toward the thought *It's my own fault*.

These brief examples are aimed at giving a glimpse of the types of things that need to be discussed during therapy. Sometimes we may believe that we do not have any of these patterns of thoughts and behaviours and it is just the tinnitus that is bothering us. This is hardly ever the case. If we are annoyed or distressed by tinnitus, and if tinnitus affects our life in some way, there is always more than just the tinnitus. In this book we will learn why we develop these patterns of thoughts and behaviours, how to identify them and, more importantly, how to change them. Reading the above examples can help us to understand how CBT might help to spot tinnitus-related negative thoughts and avoidance behaviours and how they can be changed. CBT helps us to learn alternative ways of reacting to tinnitus so as to modify the emotional disturbance caused by it. This makes it possible for the tinnitus to lose its significance and fade away into the background instead of being the centre of our attention.

The main factor that contributes to the severity of tinnitus is the annoyance it causes, rather than its loudness. This is also the case for external sounds. Sometimes we can concentrate on our work or even relax in the presence of lots of sounds. For example, an architect, engineer or a pilot can perform highly sophisticated calculations or actions when working in a noisy environment. We can relax or even fall asleep on a beach with the loud sound of the waves and other people. However, sometimes it is extremely hard to relax or concentrate in the presence of sounds that are not really loud (e.g. water dripping from a tap or the whining sound of mosquitoes). Hence, the key factor that makes it hard for us to ignore a sound, including tinnitus, is not its loudness. Rather it is the level of negative emotions it triggers. CBT can help us to explore and modify the processes that produce tinnitus-related annoyance.

During CBT we learn to understand the patterns in our behaviours, thoughts and underlying beliefs. Only then can we explore how to modify them.

Step 2. Self-assessment

It is important to self-assess our symptoms. This can help us to be more prepared when seeing a medical professional and it also can help us to make up our mind about the type of help that we should plan to seek (if needed). Step 2 provides an opportunity to develop a better understanding of the extent to which tinnitus affects our lives and of the severity of its associated symptoms, via the use of standardised self-report questionnaires.

> Self-assessment helps us to decide what kind of help we might need. Informed choices can be made once we understand our symptoms.

There are four standardised self-report questionnaires that are used in this section, comprising: (1) The Tinnitus Impact Questionnaire (TIQ); (2) The Sound Sensitivity Symptoms Questionnaire (SSSQ); (3) The Hyperacusis Impact questionnaire (HIQ); and (4) The Screening for Anxiety and Depression in Tinnitus (SAD-T). For assessment of hearing-related symptoms, a list of screening questions is used instead of a standardised questionnaire. Each questionnaire is briefly described and then presented.

Please complete all of the questionnaires in this section. Read each question carefully but do not spend too much time thinking about the answer. Choose the first answer that comes to your mind. After you have completed each questionnaire, you can calculate your total score using the key provided at the end of that questionnaire.

TIQ

This is a seven-item questionnaire asking how often you have experienced certain symptoms or effects because of tinnitus over a two-week period (14 days).

Over the last two weeks, how often would you say the following has occurred because of hearing a sound in your ears or head with no external source (e.g. buzzing, a high-pitched whistle, hissing, etc.)?				
1. Lack of concentration	0–1 days	2–6 days	7–10 days	11–14 days
2. Feeling anxious	0–1 days	2–6 days	7–10 days	11–14 days
3. Sleep difficulties (delay in falling asleep and/or difficulty getting back to sleep if woken up during the night)	0–1 nights	2–6 nights	7–10 nights	11–14 nights

4. Lack of enjoyment from leisure activities	0–1 days	2–6 days	7–10 days	11–14 days
5. Inability to perform certain day-to-day activities/tasks	0–1 days	2–6 days	7–10 days	11–14 days
6. Feeling irritable	0–1 days	2–6 days	7–10 days	11–14 days
7. Low mood	0–1 days	2–6 days	7–10 days	11–14 days

To calculate your total score, follow these instructions:

For each item, give yourself 0 points if you selected '0–1 days'; 1 point if you selected '2–6 days'; 2 points if you selected '7–10 days'; or 3 points if you selected '11–14 days'. Add the points for items 1 to 7. This gives your total score.

The total score ranges between 0 and 21. Total scores can be categorised as: (1) No tinnitus impact (TIQ score of 0 to 4); (2) Mild impact (TIQ score of 5 or 6); (3) Moderate impact (TIQ score of 7 or 8); and (4) Severe impact (TIQ score of 9 or above). Your score:

SSSQ

This five-item questionnaire measures how often you have experienced each of certain symptoms over the past two weeks. The symptoms include sound tolerance difficulties, pain or discomfort due to loud sounds, feelings of anger or anxiety upon hearing certain sounds, and a fear that certain sounds will worsen hearing or tinnitus.

Over the last two weeks, how often have you been bothered by any of the following problems?				
1. **Finding it difficult to tolerate sounds because they often seem too loud to you**	0–1 days	2–6 days	7–10 days	11–14 days
2. **Pain in your ears when hearing certain loud sounds** Examples include loud music, sirens, motorcycles, building work, lawn mowers, train stations, etc.	0–1 days	2–6 days	7–10 days	11–14 days
3. **Discomfort (physical sensations other than pain) in your ears when hearing certain loud sounds**	0–1 days	2–6 days	7–10 days	11–14 days
4. **Feeling angry or anxious when hearing certain sounds related to eating, lip smacking, sniffing, breathing, clicking sounds or tapping**	0–1 days	2–6 days	7–10 days	11–14 days
5. **Fear that certain sounds may make your hearing and/ or tinnitus worse**	0–1 days	2–6 days	7–10 days	11–14 days

For each item, give yourself 0 points if you selected '0–1 days'; 1 point if you selected '2–6 days'; 2 points if you selected '7–10 days'; or 3 points if you selected '11–14 days'. Add the points for items 1 to 5. This gives your total score. The total score ranges from 0 to 15 and scores above 4 are taken as indicating the presence of sound sensitivity. Your score:

HIQ

This questionnaire has eight items and assesses the impact of hyperacusis (oversensitivity to sound). You are asked to consider the past two weeks and to rate how often certain feelings or emotions occurred because of exposure to environmental sounds that other people could tolerate well.

Over the last two weeks, how often would you say the following have occurred because of certain environmental sounds which seemed too loud to you but people around you could tolerate well?				
1. **Feeling anxious when hearing loud noises**	0–1 days	2–6 days	7–10 days	11–14 days
2. **Avoiding certain places because it is too noisy**	0–1 days	2–6 days	7–10 days	11–14 days
3. **Lack of concentration in noisy places**	0–1 days	2–6 days	7–10 days	11–14 days
4. **Unable to relax in noisy places**	0–1 days	2–6 days	7–10 days	11–14 days

5. Difficulty in carrying out certain day-to-day activities/ tasks in noisy places	0–1 days	2–6 days	7–10 days	11–14 days
6. Lack of enjoyment from leisure activities in noisy places	0–1 days	2–6 days	7–10 days	11–14 days
7. Experiencing low mood because of your intolerance to sound	0–1 days	2–6 days	7–10 days	11–14 days
8. Getting tired quickly in noisy places	0–1 days	2–6 days	7–10 days	11–14 days

To calculate your total score, follow these instructions:

For each item, give yourself 0 points if you selected '0–1 days'; 1 point if you selected '2–6 days'; 2 points if you selected '7–10 days'; or 3 points if you selected '11–14 days'. Add the points for items 1 to 8. This gives your total score. The total score ranges from 0 to 24. Scores of 12 or more indicate a significant impact of hyperacusis. Your score:

SAD-T

The SAD-T scale contains four items taken from two well-known questionnaires, the physical health questionnaire (PHQ-9) and the generalised anxiety disorder questionnaire (GAD-7). Again, you are asked to consider the past two weeks and to rate how often certain experiences occurred. Two items are related to experiences of anxiety and worry, while another two items are related to the experience of 'anhedonia' (an inability to feel pleasure in normally pleasurable activities) and feeling 'down'.

Over the last two weeks, how often have you been bothered by the following problems?				
1. Feeling nervous, anxious or on edge	0–1 days	2–6 days	7–10 days	11–14 days
2. Not being able to stop or control worrying	0–1 days	2–6 days	7–10 days	11–14 days
3. Little interest or pleasure in doing things	0–1 days	2–6 days	7–10 days	11–14 days
4. Feeling down, depressed or hopeless	0–1 days	2–6 days	7–10 days	11–14 days

To calculate your total score, follow these instructions:

For each item, give yourself 0 points if you selected '0–1 days'; 1 point if you selected '2–6 days'; 2 points if you selected '7–10 days'; or 3 points if you selected '11–14 days'. Add the points for items 1 to 4. This gives your total score. The total score ranges from 0 to 12. Scores of 4 or more indicate possible symptoms of anxiety and/or depression. If your score is 4 or more you may need to consider seeing a mental health professional for further assessment of your symptoms and treatment if needed. Your score:

Questions relating to hearing

Do you have to ask people to repeat themselves multiple times per day?

Do you struggle to hear on the phone unless it is on speaker phone?

Do you have a hard time understanding the lyrics in songs?

Do you feel that listening requires more effort for you than for those around you?

Do you struggle to hear when there is background noise?

If your answer to any of these questions is 'yes', you should see an audiologist to have your hearing assessed.

Use the table overleaf to summarise your scores on the questionnaires and to see the extent to which tinnitus and its related symptoms are affecting you. For each questionnaire, shade the box that applies to you.

Tinnitus	
Shade this box if your total score on the TIQ is 0 to 4.	Tinnitus is not affecting me.
Shade this box if your total score on the TIQ is 5 or 6.	The impact of tinnitus on me is mild.
Shade this box if your total score on the TIQ is 7 or 8.	The impact of tinnitus on me is moderate.
Shade this box if your total score on the TIQ is 9 to 21.	The impact of tinnitus on me is severe.
Sensitivity to sound	
Shade this box if your total score on the SSSQ is 0 to 4.	I do not have symptoms of sound sensitivity.
Shade this box if your total score on the SSSQ is 5 to 15.	I may have sound sensitivity.
Hyperacusis	
Shade this box if your total score on the HIQ is less than 12.	Hyperacusis is not affecting me.
Shade this box if your total score on the HIQ is 12 or more.	Hyperacusis is affecting me.

Symptoms of anxiety and depression	
Shade this box if your total score on the SAD-T is less than 4.	I do not have symptoms of anxiety or depression.
Shade this box if your total score on the SAD-T is 4 or more.	I have symptoms of anxiety or depression.
Hearing problems	
Shade this box if you replied 'no' to all of the hearing questions.	I do not have hearing problems.
Shade this box if you replied 'yes' to any of the hearing questions.	I may have hearing problems.

For each questionnaire, if you shaded the bottom row, you may need professional help. This book can still help you but, remember, it is not a replacement for medical, audiological and psychological care.

PART II

Preparation for the Treatment

In part II, we discuss the knowledge and skills that we need to acquire prior to starting to learn CBT techniques for tinnitus management. Part II comprises Steps 3 to 5, covering the theoretical underpinnings of CBT and its relevance to tinnitus management, and how to distinguish thoughts from emotions and events, identify 'hot' thoughts, plan to tackle avoidance behaviours, learn when to use CBT skills, and enhance motivation for using CBT in managing tinnitus.

Step 3. Learn about CBT

Step 3 provides us with information about a model that characterises the mechanism by which tinnitus produces distress. This model can help us to understand the basic assumptions underlying CBT, namely the ABC model, based on theories developed by Aaron Beck and Albert Ellis. This model aims to explain the relationship between life events, our thoughts about them, and the consequential emotional and behavioural reactions.

How can CBT help?

Although it is not clear whether there is a causal relationship between anxiety and tinnitus, there is a growing body of research evidence suggesting links between them. In the absence of a cure, treatment of the depression and anxiety that are often linked to tinnitus could be beneficial. CBT is a psychological intervention that aims to alleviate anxiety by helping us to modify our dysfunctional thoughts, ruminations and safety-seeking behaviours.

In CBT, the mechanism by which tinnitus adversely affects the individual is explained with the use of models. Over the last decade, in collaboration with our psychology colleagues, we have developed several different CBT models for tinnitus distress, which were published in the *American Journal of Audiology*, the *International Journal of Audiology* and the *Journal of Psychology Research and Behaviour Management*. The models have been modified and have evolved based on experiences in clinical practice so as to be more relevant to the experience of distressing tinnitus as opposed to general anxiety. The models have also been modified so that they can be applicable to the majority of people experiencing distressing tinnitus.

In our most recent model (Figure 4), we conceptualised the distress caused by tinnitus in the following way. Tinnitus can trigger an initial reaction that includes an emotional component (e.g. feeling annoyed or irritated), bodily sensations (e.g. aural fullness or increased heart rate) and a behavioural component (e.g. rubbing the ear or changing position).

Tinnitus often resembles certain sounds that can automatically unsettle us, for example, distorted static noise, throbbing or screeching noises. These noises are often associated with something being faulty, for example a broken machine or an out of tune musical instrument. Sometimes the sounds are similar to bodily sensations that can alarm us, like heartbeats. Simply playing a recording of heartbeat sounds over headphones can induce a feeling of anxiety or fear. The association of certain sounds with painful emotions is a known phenomenon and has been cited time and again in the literature. In fact, certain sounds have been used as a symbol for emotional disturbances. For example, T.S. Eliot in his poem 'Portrait of a Lady' (1915)

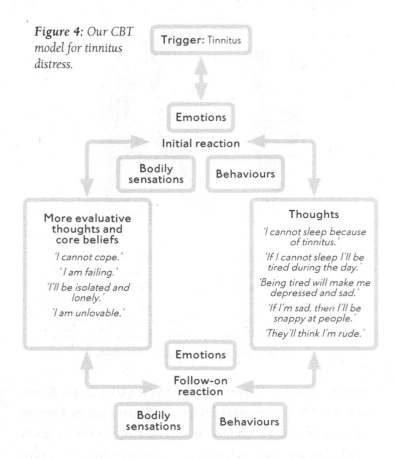

Figure 4: Our CBT model for tinnitus distress.

describes the emotional suffering and distress evoked by hearing a dull tom-tom sound hammering in his brain, a false note from cracked cornets and a capricious monotone. Dante in his *Divine Comedy* (1320) describes a scene in *Inferno* (hell) where he is violently awakened by hearing thunder rolling in his head and he describes how his ears were pierced with cries of pain.

Figure 5: *Dante Alighieri in his* Divine Comedy *(1320) described his thoughts about the nine circles of Inferno and expressed some of the terrifying emotions and thoughts he was experiencing by referring to the sounds that he heard. Some of his emotions were the immediate effect of hearing the unpleasant sounds and some were due to the meanings behind those sounds and/or his interpretations of them.*

Another example is when William Shakespeare in his *Romeo and Juliet* (1597) conveys the horror and terror felt by Juliet as hearing a shrieking sound like mandrakes torn out of the earth (mandrakes are plants whose roots have hallucinogenic properties and resemble the human body). He also portrayed the most pleasant feelings evoked when Romeo heard his lover, Juliet, calling his name: 'It is my soul that calls upon my name. How silver-sweet sound lovers' tongues by night, like softest music to attending ears!'

So, yes, hearing a sound can lead to an initial reaction prior to any conscious thought process. However, the reaction is often followed by our thoughts and appraisal of those thoughts. These thoughts are called automatic thoughts. An example of an automatic thought is *I will not be able to sleep tonight*. We talk about the characteristics of automatic thoughts in later chapters. Our thoughts lead to follow-on reactions that also have components related to emotions (e.g. fear or disappointment), behaviour (e.g. avoiding certain places or activities or seeking reassurance) and bodily sensations (tension or palpitations). The follow-on reactions may lead to further evaluative thoughts, and they may confirm our negative beliefs. These thoughts will feed back to the reactions, creating a vicious cycle of distress. When tinnitus triggers the vicious cycle, this makes it harder for our brain to push the tinnitus into the background; instead, we focus on it even more.

CBT is not aimed at reducing the perception of tinnitus. Rather, the goal is to break the vicious cycle illustrated in Figure 4, which is triggered by tinnitus. In order to break the vicious cycle, CBT is used to help us engage with our thoughts and emotions in a helpful way so that they do not lead to a snowballing effect.

> Based on our latest CBT model, the initial reaction to tinnitus (emotions, behaviours and bodily sensations) is exacerbated by negative thinking. Negative thinking causes follow-on reactions that are followed by further negative thinking and a snowballing of the initial reaction to tinnitus. This makes it harder for our brain to push tinnitus into the background.

To evaluate the effectiveness of CBT, it is necessary to compare the results for a group of people receiving CBT with the results for a matched 'control' group. The control group may receive no treatment (for example they may be put on a waiting list), in which case they are referred to as a 'passive' control group. Alternatively, the control group may receive some other form of treatment or therapy, in which case they are called an 'active' control group. There are many studies indicating that CBT is effective in alleviating the distress caused by tinnitus when compared to passive control groups and in some cases when compared to active control groups. However, not all the research studies are of the same quality in terms of the methods used, and there is a risk of bias in their results. Some studies have stronger methods and less risk of bias while other studies do not meet the highest standards of clinical research and are more prone to bias.

Meta-analysis is a statistical method that combines the results of multiple studies, taking into consideration the methodological strengths and limitations of the individual studies in order to reach an overall conclusion about the effectiveness of a treatment. A recent meta-analysis conducted by an international group of experts from the Netherlands, Germany, Belgium and the UK, published in the Cochrane Database of Systematic Reviews (2020), assessed the effect of CBT on tinnitus. The authors included twenty-eight studies on CBT for tinnitus with a total of 2,733 participants. The conclusion was that CBT was effective in reducing the negative impact of tinnitus on the patients' quality of life. Indeed, most researchers are of the opinion that the evidence supporting the effectiveness of CBT as a treatment for tinnitus distress is stronger than the evidence supporting any other form of treatment. However, CBT was usually not found to reduce the loudness of tinnitus. CBT can be effective when delivered in various formats (for example, individual face-to-face, group setting and via video or Internet). CBT can also be effective when delivered by tinnitus specialists with various professional backgrounds, including audiologists, ENT doctors, mental health professionals, social workers and teachers of the deaf.

When tinnitus no longer affects our life, it loses its significance and it is more likely to fade away into the background as opposed to staying in the focus of our attention. CBT aims to minimise the effect of tinnitus on our daily life by teaching us a certain set of skills that help us to explore and modify some of our negative thoughts about tinnitus, and to change our behaviours that follow on from those thoughts.

For many people, even if they do not receive any therapy, their tinnitus fades away into the background with the passage of time. However, this does not happen for everyone experiencing tinnitus. If you are reading this book, then it is likely that the latter applies to you. So, you may ask *Why is my tinnitus the focus of my attention and why doesn't it fade away into the background?* The information that follows might help you to understand how our brains prioritise our awareness of various sensations and the relevance of this to tinnitus.

Many types of external stimuli (stimuli that exist in the outside world) are noticed when they first occur, but if they remain steady and if they have no negative associations, awareness of them fades over time. For example, the steady background noise from a computer fan may go unnoticed after a time. This process of fading from awareness is called adaptation or habituation.

We might expect that our brain would habituate to tinnitus and it should fade into the background with the passage of time. However, if the tinnitus evokes anxiety, fear and annoyance, this can prevent the natural process of habituation. This is an evolutionary feature, which also applies to some external sounds. There is no way that our brain can get used to a sound that is interpreted as a sign of danger. For example, if there was a snake in the corner of your room, it would be impossible to ignore the sound of it hissing. Such a hissing noise is a sign of danger, and your brain would focus on it. In fact, your brain would not allow you to keep reading this book and you would have a fight-and-flight response (you would probably be on your chair screaming for help!). On the other hand, it would be possible for us to get used to such a sound if the snake was a pet and we knew that the hissing sound was normal and did not signal any danger to us.

There are several research studies indicating that the processing of emotionally significant stimuli in the brain is enhanced in comparison with the processing of neutral stimuli. This means that when tinnitus induces negative emotions, such as anxiety, fear, annoyance, anger or guilt, it is more likely to be perceived and to remain the focus of attention than if it does not evoke negative emotions. CBT assumes that the initial reaction to tinnitus is worsened as a result of our negative thoughts about tinnitus. In the next section we learn more about the interactions between thoughts and emotions and the theoretical principles of CBT.

> CBT helps us to break the cycle of distress so that the initial reaction to tinnitus does not get reinforced.
> If we reduce the response to the initial reaction by breaking the cycle, the initial reaction dies down over time. When we no longer react to tinnitus or we react less, tinnitus loses its significance and it is more likely to fade into the background as opposed to staying the focus of our attention.

Learning about the effect of thoughts on emotions

Figure 6: Aristotle and the Greek Stoics believed that happiness depended on human judgements about things that affected them.

The philosophical underpinnings of CBT can be traced back thousands of years to the time of the Greek Stoics in the third century BC, who believed that destructive emotions result from errors in judgement. Similarly, the Roman Emperor Marcus Aurelius said 'If thou art pained by any external thing, it is not this thing that disturbs thee, but thine own judgement about it. And it is in thy power to wipe out this judgement now'. Everyone experiences thoughts that they believe are true but are in fact unrealistic and not representative of the true situation. Aristotle is quoted as saying 'the arousing of prejudice, pity, anger and similar emotions has nothing to do with the essential facts, but is merely a personal appeal to the man who is judging the case.' So our emotional reactions to life events do not reflect literal facts but are a reflection of our interpretation of those events. Concepts consistent with CBT have also been presented by Eastern scholars, including the thirteenth-century Persian poet Jalāl ad-Dīn Mohammad Balkhī, known as Rumi in the West. For example, in his poem 'Elephant in the dark room,' Rumi talks about how our limited perspectives and errors of thoughts lead to us feeling cynical about events and life in general, and he argues that by changing and broadening our perspectives we can brighten our mind's dark room. However, CBT as we know it today is based on the works of the American psychologists Aaron Beck and Albert Ellis, also known as the father and grandfather of CBT.

The ABC model is one way of describing the principles of CBT. It is aimed at explaining the relationship between our environment, what we think, how we feel and what we do.

A represents Activating events or situations.

B represents Beliefs or underlying thoughts.

C represents the Consequences or reactions, which may be emotional, behavioural or physiological.

Figure 7 illustrates the ABC model.

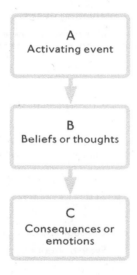

Figure 7: The ABC model.

According to the ABC model, our reactions to life events are the result of our interpretations of and thoughts about those events. In our day-to-day experience, we often notice events and their corresponding effect on how we feel and what we do. However, we do not necessarily recognise the underlying thought processes that link the events and our reactions. The ABC model highlights the role of our thoughts in influencing the effect that an event can have on us. In order to use CBT as a tinnitus self-management technique, it is important to be able to distinguish between Activating events, Beliefs or thoughts, and Consequences, such as our emotions and behaviours. Here are some general ABC examples:

A
Activating event:
A doctor is stuck in traffic and there are lots of patients waiting for him in the hospital

B
Belief:
Patients will blame me for being late and they will complain to my boss

C
Consequence:
Feeling anxious

Figure 8: Example of the ABC model.

In Figure 8, the Activating event (A) is the fact that a doctor is stuck in traffic. If he thinks that he will be blamed (B) then he will feel anxious (C). Let's change his thoughts in two different directions, firstly to make him even more anxious and perhaps fearful and secondly to help him to feel less anxious in the exact same scenario. In other words, we are going to change B with no change in A and see what happens to C.

Figure 9 illustrates the effect of changing B and consequently C for the worse.

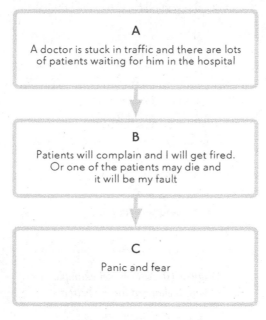

A
A doctor is stuck in traffic and there are lots of patients waiting for him in the hospital

B
Patients will complain and I will get fired. Or one of the patients may die and it will be my fault

C
Panic and fear

Figure 9: ABC model example
with B changed for the worse.

Figure 10 illustrates the effect of changing B and consequently C for the better.

Figure 10: ABC model example
with B changed for the better.

In the above scenario, feeling anxious and panicky may affect the person's behaviour and increase the likelihood that they make mistakes in their driving, which in turn may make a bad situation even worse. So, the feeling of anxiety is not at all helpful to this individual; rather, it would be better if they were able to change their thoughts so that they felt calmer, even though the scenario remained the same.

Figure 11 gives another example:

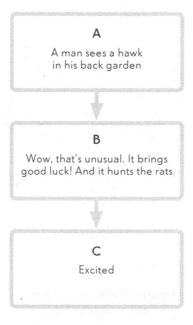

Figure 11: ABC model example with positive beliefs.

In this example, the Activating event (A) is the fact that a man sees a bird of prey. If he thinks that it brings good luck (B) then he will feel excited (C). Let's change his thoughts to make him feel frightened in the same scenario. We will only change B with no change in A, and we will see what happens to C (Figure 12).

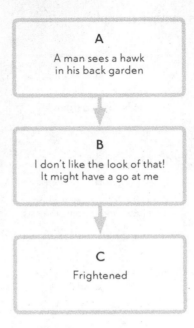

*Figure 12: ABC model example
with a negative belief.*

Figure 13 illustrates a noise-related ABC example.

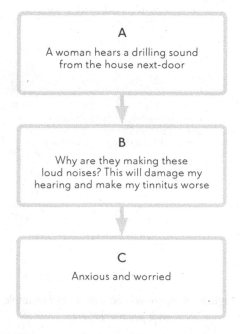

Figure 13: Noise-related ABC model example with negative beliefs.

In this example, the Activating event (A) is hearing a drilling sound made by a neighbour. If the thought is that it will make her tinnitus worse (B), she will feel anxious (C). The anxiety (C) itself can make the tinnitus louder, which she takes as proof of the validity of her thoughts (B), a self-fulfilling prophecy.

Let's change her thoughts to help her feel less worried in the same scenario. We will just change B with no change in A and we will see what happens to C.

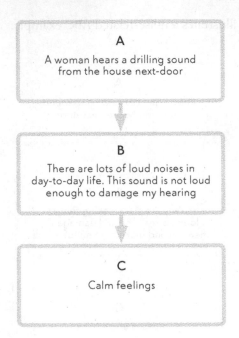

Figure 14: Noise-related ABC model example with positive beliefs.

Here is a tinnitus-related ABC example:

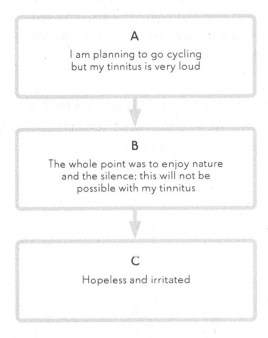

*Figure 15: Tinnitus-related ABC model example
with negative beliefs.*

In this example, the Activating event (A) is hearing loud tinnitus. This reduces the person's motivation for going cycling. If they think that tinnitus will spoil their enjoyment (B) then they feel irritated and hopeless (C). This may affect their behaviour, making them abandon the idea of cycling. This in turn may lead to the thought that there is nothing in life that they can enjoy any more. The behaviour of not going cycling will be taken as proof of the validity of their thoughts, a self-fulfilling prophecy.

According to the ABC model, the reason that we feel annoyed, anxious, irritated, restless, depressed . . . is not hearing the tinnitus but rather our thoughts about it.

Let's change his thoughts to help him feel more hopeful in the same scenario. We will only change B with no change in A and we will see what happens to C.

A
I am planning to go cycling but my tinnitus is very loud

B
Cycling gives me a sense of freedom. The physical activity makes my muscles feel good. Fresh air is good for me. I can enjoy all of this despite my tinnitus

C
Hopefulness and optimism

Figure 16: Tinnitus-related ABC model example with positive beliefs.

The ABC model is based on the idea that the reason for reactions such as annoyance or anxiety is not the tinnitus itself but is instead the negative thoughts we have about the tinnitus. The emotional reaction we have to tinnitus makes it difficult for our brains to push it into the background, as the brain usually does with many different bodily noises and environmental sounds. It is helpful to remember that our emotions can also affect our thoughts. All of us have experienced the effect of our emotions on our thoughts at some time during our lives. For example, when we are angry or depressed, our thought processes are different compared with the times when we feel calm and content. That's why it is said 'Don't make important decisions when you are angry'. This is also the case when we experience strong positive emotions. For example, we might not think sensibly when we are very excited, or we may have very rash thoughts when we are in love!

CBT can help us to identify our negative thoughts about tinnitus and to modify them. It also helps us to consider, *Am I thinking this way because I am feeling nervous/angry/excited? Would I think about this in the same way if I felt differently?* Once the tinnitus-induced annoyance or anxiety is minimised with the use of CBT techniques, tinnitus can lose its significance and fade away into the background. CBT can also help us to become aware of what we tend to do when tinnitus is bothering us, and to consider whether these actions are helpful in managing our tinnitus. CBT helps us to test new ways of acting that may be more helpful for us in the long-term.

But is CBT really for us? The next chapter will help us to decide!

Step 4. Test the Water!

Before fully committing to CBT, we need to 'test the water'. Step 4 provides an opportunity for us to: (1) practise developing the skills needed to identify our key troublesome thoughts, also known as *hot* thoughts; (2) understand how some of our instinctive behaviours can be counterproductive; (3) develop a plan for tackling our troublesome thoughts and unhelpful behaviours; and (4) learn when to use CBT skills. All these are introductory CBT skills. Learning about them will help us to decide if CBT is the way forward or if we prefer not to embark on this journey. Step 4 helps us to make an informed choice as to whether or not to undertake CBT.

Practise identifying *hot* thoughts

To prepare for CBT, it is important to develop the skill of identifying our key troublesome tinnitus-related thoughts, also known as *hot* thoughts. The term *hot* thoughts is used to describe thoughts that, compared to other thoughts, produce a lot of undesirable emotions. One of the key CBT skills is to identify our *hot* thoughts and modify them. Identifying *hot* thoughts is a good skill to learn in the preparation stage, because it gives us a sense of how it would feel to undertake CBT. This is because in CBT we need to classify our thoughts and their effects on our emotions. This prepares us for more complex tasks ahead. There are two things that we need to cover before we start learning about *hot* thoughts. The first is to practise identifying the events, thoughts and emotions that we learned about in the previous section. The second is to practise noticing our mood when we are bothered by tinnitus and to identify what goes through our mind about tinnitus. After we have identified our thoughts, we can practise deciding which ones are *hot* thoughts.

The worksheet below can be used for practice. Write down in the right column whether the item in the left column is an event, thought or emotion. The first three rows are completed for you, as examples.

Item	Event, thought or emotion?
Anger.	Emotion
Hearing a loud noise at workplace.	Event
If I hear my tinnitus, I will not be able to concentrate.	Thought
Tinnitus will ruin my day.	
Noticing tinnitus when going to bed.	

Anxiety.	
Fear.	
Sadness.	
Tinnitus gets louder after being at a party.	
I will never have peace and quiet.	
Mishearing conversations in noisy places.	
Tinnitus is a terrible disease.	
I cannot cope.	
I will not be able to enjoy certain activities.	
Noticing tinnitus when trying to relax.	
I will never be able to relax or chill out.	
I will be able to cope.	
I must change my job in order to deal with tinnitus.	
I am resilient so I can manage this problem.	
I am a failure.	
Watching TV and hearing tinnitus.	
Irritation.	
I am a loser.	

Depression.	
Happiness.	
Feeling confident.	
Driving my car and tinnitus seemed very quiet.	
While walking with a friend in the park, I could hear my tinnitus in the background.	
Tinnitus will make me a stronger person.	
Tinnitus makes me crazy.	
Feeling content.	

Now that we have practised distinguishing thoughts, emotions and events, we can start learning the next skill. This is to learn how to track our mood when tinnitus is bothering us and to identify what goes through our mind about tinnitus. Before moving on to the next step, see the answers for the thoughts, emotions and events quiz in the table overleaf. If you feel that you are not fully ready to distinguish thoughts, emotions and events, then please review the section on 'Learning about the effect of thoughts on emotions' (page 93). This can help you to enhance this skill, which is a prerequisite to learning how to undertake CBT.

Here are the answers.

Item	Event, thought or emotion?
Anger.	Emotion
Hearing a loud noise at workplace.	Event
If I hear my tinnitus, I will not be able to concentrate.	Thought
Tinnitus will ruin my day.	Thought
Noticing tinnitus when going to bed.	Event
Anxiety.	Emotion
Fear.	Emotion
Sadness.	Emotion
Tinnitus gets louder after being at a party.	Event
I will never have peace and quiet.	Thought
Mishearing conversations in noisy places.	Event
Tinnitus is a terrible disease.	Thought
I cannot cope.	Thought
I will not be able to enjoy certain activities.	Thought
Noticing tinnitus when trying to relax.	Event

I will never be able to relax or chill out.	Thought
I will be able to cope.	Thought
I must change my job in order to deal with tinnitus.	Thought
I am resilient so I can manage this problem.	Thought
I am a failure.	Thought
Watching TV and hearing tinnitus.	Event
Irritation.	Emotion
I am a loser.	Thought
Depression.	Emotion
Happiness.	Emotion
Feeling confident.	Emotion
Driving my car and tinnitus seemed very quiet.	Event
While walking with a friend in the park, I could hear my tinnitus in the background.	Event
Tinnitus will make me a stronger person.	Thought
Tinnitus makes me crazy.	Thought
Feeling content.	Emotion

To practise tracking our mood at times when tinnitus is bothering us and to identify what goes through our mind about tinnitus, we can use the Tinnitus, Mood and Thoughts (TMT) worksheet, which appears opposite. It is best to complete the TMT each time when your tinnitus is bothersome, or, failing that, very soon afterwards. It can be very difficult to recall your mood or what you were thinking if you do not make a note of these at the time when they happened. In the first column, write down what is happening and when it is. How loud is the tinnitus? Where are you? Who are you with? In the second column, write down your mood. In the third column, write down what is going through your mind about tinnitus. An example is given on the next page.

Example: Tinnitus, Mood and Thoughts worksheet (TMT)

Tinnitus-related event	Mood	Thoughts
When? What? How loud is my tinnitus on a scale from 0 to 10? (0 means no tinnitus and 10 means extreme loudness) Where? Who?		
It is Sunday 5 pm, I am watching my favourite TV show, tinnitus is loud 7/10, I cannot enjoy the programme, and I am with Sue.	What is my mood? Irritated	What is going through my mind about my tinnitus right now? Damn this noise, I can't enjoy watching TV. I will never have a normal life.

Use the TMT worksheet opposite to practise describing events, mood and thoughts before moving on to practising the next skill, which is identifying your *hot* thoughts. For this assignment, you need to enter five tinnitus-related events, your mood at the time and your thoughts for each one. You can complete this in one day or several days.

After learning how to take note of tinnitus-related events, moods and your thoughts, you may be ready to try to identify your *hot* thoughts. To recap, these are thoughts that are directly linked with your emotional reactions to various life events, including tinnitus. *Hot* thoughts are the thoughts that cause strong negative emotions in response to tinnitus. It is important to identify these thoughts, examine them and modify them if you decide that they are unhelpful or irrational. Modifying *hot* thoughts can directly change our emotional reactions to tinnitus without any change in the tinnitus itself. It is important to develop the skill of distinguishing *hot* thoughts from other negative thoughts.

> *Hot* thoughts are thoughts that, compared to other thoughts, produce the greatest undesirable emotions when we think about them.

Recall that if tinnitus induces negative emotions, such as anxiety, fear, annoyance, anger or guilt, the tinnitus is more likely to be perceived and to remain the focus of attention than if it does not evoke negative emotions. In future steps we will learn methods

TMT worksheet

Tinnitus-related Event	Mood	Thoughts
When? What? How loud is my tinnitus on a scale from 0 to 10? (0 means no tinnitus and 10 means extreme loudness) Where? Who?	What is my mood?	What is going through my mind about my tinnitus right now?

for effectively modifying such negative thoughts. But at this stage it is vital to gain more understanding about how to identify these thoughts. The Tinnitus Hot Thoughts (THT) worksheet can be used to practise identifying your *hot* thoughts. As with the TMT, it is best to complete the THT each time when your tinnitus is bothersome, or, failing that, very soon afterwards.

There are four steps in completing the THT worksheet:

Step 1: Make a note of the situation where your tinnitus is causing difficulty for you. This is similar to the tinnitus-related events that we practised in the previous section. You need to add some description to cover When? What? How loud is the tinnitus on a scale from 0 to 10? Where? and Who?

Step 2: Write down your mood at that moment.

Step 3: Ask yourself: What is going through my mind about my tinnitus right now? Why does that matter to me? What is the worst that can happen? What images or memories come to my mind in such situations? This is similar to identifying the thoughts that we practised in the TMT.

Step 4: To identify your *hot* thoughts, you need to rate how much anxiety or other undesirable emotions each thought alone produces. The thoughts that produce the greatest undesirable emotions are your *hot* thoughts.

While steps 1 to 3 need to be done at the time when your tinnitus is bothersome, or as soon as possible afterwards, step 4 can be done whenever you have time to do it.

An example is given on pages 118–119.

In this example, the first thought 'Damn this noise, I can't enjoy watching TV' did not produce a lot of negative feelings, so it is not classified as a *hot* thought. The second and fourth thoughts ('It means that I cannot enjoy anything because of this for the rest of my life,' and 'Memory of my mum who suffered badly from depression. . .') produced medium levels of negative feelings so they were hotter than the first thought. The third thought, 'My life is ruined. I will end up isolated, depressed and sad' produced the highest level of negative feelings. Hence it was the *hot* thought. Asking ourselves some questions about the meaning behind our thoughts and what we are afraid of can help to identify our *hot* thoughts, as demonstrated in this example.

Past memories of family members or close friends who might have struggled in coping with health conditions, can make it more likely for us to have thoughts that if tinnitus gets worse then we won't be able to manage it. In the above example, memories about a mother who developed dementia were closely related to anxiety responses evoked by tinnitus. Identifying such memories can be helpful during therapy, as we can think of differences between our current circumstances and the circumstances in our memories. This can help to modify our reactions to tinnitus.

Another example of the THT is given on page 120–1:

THT worksheet example

Tinnitus-related difficulty	What is my mood/emotion right now?	Tinnitus-related thoughts:	How much does each thought produce negative feelings, on a scale from 0–100% (0 = not at all)
It is Sunday 5 pm, I am watching my favourite TV show, tinnitus is loud 7/10, I cannot enjoy the programme, and I am with Sue.	Anxious	What is going through my mind about my tinnitus right now?	
		Damn this noise, I can't enjoy watching TV.	10%
		Why does that matter to me?	
		It means that I cannot enjoy anything because of this for the rest of my life.	40%

What is the worst that can happen to me?	90%
My life is ruined. I will end up isolated, depressed and sad.	
What images or memories come to my mind in such a situation?	40%
Memory of my mum who suffered badly from depression. Then developed dementia. Very sad. I do not want to end up like that.	

THT worksheet example

Tinnitus-related difficulty	What is my mood/emotion right now?	Tinnitus-related thoughts:	How much does each thought produce negative feelings, on a scale from 0–100% (0 = not at all)
It is Monday 10 am, I am reading a book and my tinnitus is bothering me. My tinnitus is loud, 8/10	Frustration	What is going through my mind about my tinnitus right now? Because I feel frustrated, I will not be able to read my book.	60%
		Why does that matter to me? Tinnitus affects everything that I want to do.	40%

What is the worst that can happen to me? *I will never be happy.*	90%
If that's true, what does it mean to me? *I am failing.*	90%
What images or memories come to my mind in such a situation? *Memories of all the times that I failed in my life. This proves that I am a failure.*	90%

In the TMT on pages 120–121, the thoughts 'Because I feel frustrated, I will not be able to read my book' and 'Tinnitus affects everything that I want to do' were given 60 per cent and 40 per cent ratings for negative emotions, respectively. In contrast, the thoughts 'I will never be happy' and 'I am failing' were given 90 per cent ratings for negative emotions, indicating that they are *hot* thoughts.

The thought 'I will never be happy' has at least two problems associated with it. Firstly, it is an exaggeration of the problem. If a person cannot read due to the distraction produced by their tinnitus at a given time, this does not mean that they will never be happy. Secondly, this person may have a belief that they must always be happy, so they become frustrated and upset by a thought that tells them exactly the opposite. It is not realistic to think that one always needs to be happy, because we have a wide range of emotions from happiness to sadness and all need to be felt at different times. In addition, this person seems to have a lack of tolerance for negative feelings and interprets them as a sign of failure. This is apparent in their other *hot* thought 'I am failing'. This suggests a general sense of failure, which is an all-or-nothing thinking error. Failing is a part of our life experiences. We learn how to change our behaviour when we fail, and failing in a specific task does not mean that we are a failure in general. During therapy, this person recognised that it was not true that they were a failure. They were able to identify things they had done in their life that were a success. They recognised that they had achieved many things in their life and that everyone has successes and failures. In a later chapter we will learn more about how to identify and challenge biased thinking. However, at this stage the task is to explore our thoughts and assess the extent of the negative emotions they produce.

Another example can be found overleaf. In the example, 'I am weak' was identified as a *hot* thought. The person could relate this belief to childhood memories of growing up in an environment where he was never praised. During the therapy sessions he reflected on all the things that he had achieved throughout his life. Based on these he modified this thought to 'I have weaknesses and strengths'. He also shifted his thoughts from being centred about himself to the bigger context of reality for all human beings by changing his thought 'I am vulnerable' to 'Vulnerability is a fact of life for humans'. These changes made it much easier for him to be willing to live with his tinnitus and the negative emotions caused by it. Willingness to live with tinnitus made his emotional reactions to it less bothersome. The less he was bothered by his emotions, the less he noticed them, and the more confident he became in leading a normal life, even when hearing tinnitus.

THT worksheet example

Tinnitus-related difficulty	How does it make me feel?	Tinnitus-related thoughts	How much does each thought produce negative feelings, on a scale from 0–100% (0 = not at all)
When? What? How loud is my tinnitus on a scale from 0 to 10? Where? Who?	*Emotion*	*What is going through my mind about tinnitus right now? Why does that matter to me? What is the worst that can happen? What images or memories come to my mind in such a situation?*	
It is Tuesday 2 am, I woke up noticing my tinnitus, which is loud, 8/10	Panicky and claustrophobic	What is going through my mind about tinnitus right now?

I'm going to have to deal with this for the rest of my life. | 30% |
| | | Why does that matter to me?

I cannot enjoy my life fully. | 30% |

What is the worst that can happen to me? *I will become depressed.* If that's true, what does it mean to me? *I am weak/vulnerable*	*75%* *90%*
What images or memories come to my mind in such a situation? *My father never praised me. All my childhood and later in life I had this feeling that I was not good enough.*	*90%*

Figure 17: Rumi (1207–73) believed that if we change our viewpoint from being centred on ourselves even for one moment, we will learn things that are hidden to us: 'If you could get rid of yourself just once, the secret of secrets would open to you.'

The willingness to be aware of our vulnerabilities and weaknesses without judging them is a key concept in CBT and related therapies such as mindfulness, dialectical behaviour therapy, and acceptance and commitment therapy. This concept is fundamentally identical to the teachings of Buddhism and Sufism that focus on experiencing existence instead of questioning it. There are many references to Buddhist philosophy in the modern psychology literature, but not many references to Sufism. To gain a more balanced view, here we give an example of the concept of acceptance in Sufism, especially from the works of Rumi. Rumi considered acceptance as an act of courage and a way to gain insight. Here is one of his poems:

This being human is a guest house, every morning a new arrival. A joy, a depression, a meanness, some momentary awareness comes as an unexpected visitor. Welcome and entertain them all! Even if they are a crowd of sorrows, who violently sweep your house empty of its furniture. Still treat each guest honourably. They may be clearing you out for some new delight.

These concepts help to change our perspectives about the problems that we may be experiencing and to move away from being centred on ourselves. In later chapters we discuss in more detail how to modify negative thoughts and to apply the principles of acceptance in the management of tinnitus.

Use the THT worksheet on the next page to list some of your thoughts about tinnitus and the consequent emotions. Rate how much undesirable emotion each thought produces. Identify your *hot* thought. For this assignment you need to complete all four rows.

As mentioned earlier, this needs to be done at the moment that your tinnitus is bothering you or as soon as possible afterwards.

THT worksheet

Tinnitus-related difficulty *When? What? How loud is my tinnitus on a scale from 0 to 10? Where? Who?*	How does it make me feel? *Emotion*	Tinnitus-related thoughts *What is going through my mind about tinnitus right now? Why does that matter to me? What is the worst that can happen? What images or memories come to my mind in such a situation?*	Rating Rate how much each thought produced negative feelings, on a scale from 0–100% (0 = not at all)

> To do CBT, it is important to dig deeper in our
> thoughts and identify thoughts that bother us the
> most. If we do not know them then we won't be able
> to change them!

Identifying our negative thoughts and trying to change them can be difficult tasks. When we first identify our negative thoughts, it may make us feel worse. These are upsetting thoughts and naturally we might not wish to think about them. Trying to stop our thoughts can also produce some anxiety. It is often very difficult to stop thinking about something, especially when it is important to us. At this stage, the task is to simply to build up the skill of identifying our thoughts and emotions and distinguishing them from one another. We are at the preparation stage. In the next chapter we discuss methods for modifying our negative thoughts.

Going against our instinct

Often, we try to change our behaviour in ways that we think might protect us from having unwanted experiences. For example, we might believe 'I cannot enjoy the cinema because my tinnitus will be too distracting'. So we decide to stop going to the cinema and never go again. We conclude that the cinema will never be enjoyable because of tinnitus. We might even feel some relief about our decision to stop going and feel a short-term reduction in stress and anxiety. However, this thought may not be true. We may be able to enjoy the cinema just as much as anything else, even if our tinnitus is there. We may be over-estimating the likelihood that we will not enjoy ourselves because of tinnitus if we go to the cinema. But, if we never go back to the cinema again, we never have the chance to learn that the opposite may be true. Instead, we think that we are managing our tinnitus by using this avoidance behaviour. The difficulties with avoidance behaviours are that they can lead to a lot of restrictions in the way that we live our lives, they can take a lot of time and effort to maintain and, ultimately, they keep us from learning that the beliefs that we have might not actually be true.

Another example of avoidance behaviour is listening to background music in order to distract ourselves from tinnitus while at work or when going to bed at night. Although listening to background music sporadically may help in reducing the annoyance of tinnitus and its effect on us in the short term, such avoidance behaviour can backfire in the long run. You may question this concept. You may feel that listening to soothing music takes the edge off your tinnitus and helps you to cope better. Although this may seem like a reasonable solution when tinnitus is irritating, it can make us believe that if we do not listen to music then we will not be able to cope as well. This belief can make us feel further annoyed by our tinnitus, which can lead to greater perception of it in the long term. Furthermore, some people believe that using distraction techniques can give a temporary sense of control over their tinnitus, helping them to deal with the fear of not having control over it. However, most people realise that this is a false perception since tinnitus is never fully under our control. The right solution is to work on the importance that we give to control of tinnitus, or the lack of it. This is discussed in the next section.

Avoidance is a human instinct, and it comes to us naturally to help us deal with unpleasant experiences. Avoidance is a legitimate coping method that we can utilise when facing problems that we can't resolve. However, what comes to us naturally does not necessarily represent the best course of action in a given scenario. For example, if we have back pain, whenever our back hurts we naturally feel that we should lie down and relax. However, when we see a physiotherapist, they may tell us that we have to move and do back exercises even when our back is hurting. The physiotherapist is likely to say that we need to strengthen some of our back muscles and other core muscles with the use of exercises. This may hurt initially, but once the muscles are strengthened, we will have less back pain. This is completely contrary to our instinctive reaction of wanting to rest whenever our back hurts. Another example demonstrating that our first instinct may not be the best course of action is the instinct to run away when we see a mountain lion while out hiking. If we run, this only encourages the mountain lion to attack. The best strategy is to stay still but to make yourself look at big as possible by standing tall and raising your arms over your head. If you do this, after a while, the mountain lion will probably decide that you are too big for it to risk an attack, and it will retreat. So, what comes naturally is not always the best course of action.

You may ask what is wrong with having a little help? If I have a headache, I will take a painkiller, so why shouldn't I listen to background sounds when I have tinnitus? But think again about the situation with the mountain lion. Running away may feel like the only solution that we have at the time. But if we run, and for some reason are not attacked, we will never learn that it would actually have been safer to stand tall and raise our arms. Similarly, if we consistently deal with a headache by taking a painkiller, we may fail to realise that our headaches are actually caused by eyestrain and that we need a new prescription for our glasses. So, although we may think that dealing with tinnitus by using background music or other avoidance techniques is the only solution, the use of such techniques can prevent us from learning how to manage tinnitus without being dependent on them.

Some may counter argue that if I have a disability and can't walk well, then I should use a stick. Similarly, why shouldn't I use some noise or music if it distracts me from my tinnitus and helps me to do what I need to do? But suppose that you don't actually need to use a stick. What if your chance of falling over is actually very low and it is your fear of falling over that makes you use the stick? The stick may seem like a harmless way of helping you to walk. But can you run with the stick in your hand? Could the stick make your life restricted if you keep using it when you don't need to? Tinnitus is not like a broken leg that can heal while in a cast or a cut that you can cover with a plaster while it heals. Instead of attempting to avoid tinnitus, we need to learn how to function well, rest and relax, and enjoy life even when hearing it. If we achieve this, then tinnitus loses its significance and becomes much easier to cope with.

So, in order to manage tinnitus and the distress it causes, we should spend time with it instead of avoiding it. Remember that our anxieties and fears about the effects of tinnitus are not based on facts and they may prove to be untrue when we spend time with tinnitus and have developed a willingness to live our life fully even with tinnitus. In the next section we start some preparatory work for tackling our avoidance behaviours. But let's elaborate on the issue of acceptance a little bit more.

> Avoiding tinnitus and the distress it causes is not a long-term solution. We need to face our fears as a key step in tinnitus management.

The French fairy tale *Beauty and the Beast*, described earlier, seems very relevant to the idea of acceptance. Beauty had to accept the Beast as a beast, which naturally was hard and counter-intuitive. But by doing so the Beast was transformed into a prince. Beauty did not know that by falling in love with the Beast it would turn into a prince. So the problem for her was to accept the Beast wholeheartedly, with no ifs or buts or a hidden agenda.

Figure 18: *In the fairy tale* Beauty and the Beast, *Beauty had to accept the Beast as a beast. We should accept ourselves as who we are right now even in our low moments with tinnitus. This is likely to remove the barriers to improving our situation and reaching our goals.*

Sometimes patients ask, 'If I accept my tinnitus, will it become quieter?' This is like Beauty asking whether the Beast will turn into a prince if she accepts it. But this was not what happened or what was required. Beauty accepted the Beast as a beast without expecting it to turn into a prince. This is just a metaphor for acceptance. Tinnitus will not become quieter or disappear altogether just because we have accepted it. Rather, if we accept ourselves as who we are even at difficult moments of experiencing tinnitus, we remove barriers for recovery and self-growth so that we actually can get to the place where we want to be as a person. Acceptance is an alternative to avoidance and is in fact a principal component of certain CBT therapies, such as acceptance and commitment therapy. In later chapters we will learn more about the acceptance of tinnitus as opposed to using avoidance behaviours.

> Acceptance is an alternative to avoidance. Although acceptance is often harder than avoidance, when we accept tinnitus (with true acceptance, like Beauty accepting the Beast), positive changes will follow. Acceptance can release resources that were previously used in the battle with tinnitus, which can instead be used to enjoy our lives.

The actual behaviour or action that is used to alleviate tinnitus may be completely harmless or even useful. The context is very important in understanding if a certain action is part of an avoidance or ritualist behaviour or if it is just a sensible and useful behaviour. For example, if we have hearing difficulties and we do not use hearing aids in the fear that they may make our tinnitus worse, then this would be classified as an avoidance behaviour, because the use of hearing aids in this situation would be a useful and sensible behaviour. If, on the other hand, we do not have hearing difficulties, then the use of hearing aids in an attempt to alleviate tinnitus would be classified as a ritualistic behaviour. Other examples are taking exercise, cutting down on alcohol, reducing sugar consumption and stopping smoking. All these have health benefits and are surely recommended. However, if we do them in order to reduce tinnitus or distract ourselves from it, they will become like avoidance and ritualistic behaviours, which would be counterproductive for managing tinnitus.

Let us give an example in order to make this crystal clear. Washing our hands with soap and water after going to the toilet is a basic principle of personal hygiene. It is even more important to wash our hands after going to the toilet if we are about to eat food. But does this depend on the context? Can it be taken too far? Consider a person with obsessive compulsive disorder (OCD) who keeps washing their hands to the point that they become red and raw and bleed. This behaviour is often a result of their fear of contamination. One aim of the treatment is to get them to stop this behaviour via exposure to the fear. In this example, the person with OCD has to refrain from washing their hands after going to the toilet and has to eat their food without washing their hands. Although this sounds gross, the risk is actually minimal. After all, most young children touch things that they shouldn't and put their hands in their mouth frequently! They usually survive, don't they? For the person with OCD, overcoming the fear of contamination is far more important than the possibility of germs making them sick. Consistent with this, facing our fears about tinnitus is more important than any possible improvement in our hearing produced by using hearing aids, having a good diet, and leading a healthy lifestyle. Of course, we can always do all these once we have faced our fears and provided that we are not adopting these behaviours to try to alleviate our tinnitus.

> The more we change our life because of tinnitus, the more important the tinnitus becomes.

Another important thing to bear in mind is that when we stop some avoidance behaviours, we should not replace them with others. For example, we may have a negative thought that *I cannot sleep because of my tinnitus* and the relevant avoidance behaviour could be to use music or soothing background sounds at night for distraction or to mask the tinnitus. In order to face our fear, we need to stop the avoidance behaviour and go to bed at night without using any background sound. However, if we try to calm ourselves in other ways, such as by using deep breathing, counting backwards or going to bed very late, we are still avoiding facing our fear. The types of techniques that we may use to calm ourselves when exposed to the feared scenario are known as rituals. Although rituals may seem to be the only way that we can deal with tinnitus at the time, they do not let us properly test our negative thoughts to see if they are true. Hence the rituals jeopardise the purpose of the exposure. The problem with using rituals during exposure is that instead of changing the negative thought to *I can sleep even if I hear my tinnitus* we may think *I can sleep when I hear tinnitus only if I do deep breathing or calm myself or if I am very tired* . . . This does not make the tinnitus insignificant, which is the aim of the therapy. So it is important to stop rituals as well as avoidance behaviours when facing our fears.

Overcoming our avoidance behaviours and rituals can be an anxiety-provoking process because we need to stop some of our behaviours and expose ourselves to our fears. For some of us, stress and anxiety by themselves can make tinnitus seem worse, which may lead us to go back to our safety-seeking behaviours when we try something new. However, it is known that over time, if we experience the same event repeatedly without negative consequences (a process we call exposure), we will feel less stress and anxiety and our brains will start to get used to these events or may stop noticing them almost entirely (a process called habituation). At this stage we only need to prepare ourselves to identify our avoidance behaviours. Once we learn more about our behaviours and rituals, we may feel more ready to minimise them, but not just yet.

Planning to tackle our avoidance behaviours

There are various methods that people use to try to avoid tinnitus. Often people have negative predictions about what might happen to them when they became aware of their tinnitus and do not have any means of distracting themselves from it. As a result, they take precautions to prevent these negative predictions from happening. These precautions often take the form of avoidance behaviours. In order to manage tinnitus using this self-help book, we need to drop some of these behaviours so that we are exposed to our feared scenarios. Once we are exposed to the feared scenarios, we can test the validity of our predictions and assess whether the precautions were justified.

Exposing ourselves to our feared scenarios can also improve our tolerance for tinnitus and for the uncomfortable feelings that it may cause.

We may find the prospect of being exposed to our feared scenarios stressful and feel ambivalent about reducing our avoidance behaviours. It is understandable to feel that way. There are several reasons that people give for not wanting to abandon their avoidance behaviours, including: (1) fear of causing further damage, for example we may fear that environmental noise will damage our hearing or will make our tinnitus worse; (2) fear of experiencing certain emotions that we do not like, for example we may fear becoming very upset and agitated; (3) fear of the impact on our job, day-to-day tasks, relationships and sleep, for example we may fear that if we do not use background noise/music when going to bed at night, we will sleep very badly, which will affect our activities the following day. All these may make us think 'I cannot do it!'

In this step we discuss some ideas that you might find helpful in planning how to tackle avoidance behaviours. The decision as to whether or not to change certain behaviours is entirely up to you. No one can make such decisions for you, even if they wanted to. In this section, we simply discuss a few ideas in case you do decide to make some positive changes. But, yes, the decision is yours!

Planning to reduce our avoidance behaviours and rituals is a vital component of the preparation stage in this ten-step self-help guide.

The first stage is to create a list of behaviours that you might identify as tinnitus-related avoidance behaviours. This is called the exposure menu. The exposure menu overleaf is an example that includes typical tinnitus-related avoidance behaviours. You may use the blank exposure menu worksheet for tinnitus to write down avoidance behaviours based on your own personal experiences with tinnitus. The behaviour column is dedicated to the actual behaviour (e.g. always having music in the background when reading). In the next column you need to write down your reasons for this behaviour. Ask yourself what would happen if you did not adhere to that behaviour. For example, what would happen if you did not use music in the background when you were reading? You may think that you would be upset and restless due to the tinnitus and you would not be able to enjoy reading. Write this down in the column labelled 'What is the fear leading to this behaviour?'. In the last column you need to rate how difficult it would be for you if you did drop that particular behaviour. For example, how difficult would it be for you to enjoy reading your book if you did not use background music? Rate the anticipated difficulty from 0 per cent 'not difficult at all' to 100 per cent 'extreme difficulty to the point that it would be impossible to enjoy the book'.

Example of an Exposure Menu for Tinnitus worksheet

Exposure Menu for Tinnitus			
Item	Behaviour	What is the fear leading to this behaviour?	How difficult is it for me to stop this behaviour? *Rate the difficulty from 0% 'not difficult at all' to 100% 'impossible'.*
1	I always have music in the background when reading	If I do not use background music I will get upset and restless due to my tinnitus and I will not be able to enjoy reading.	50%
2	Not going to parties	Noise makes my tinnitus worse, and I will not be able to enjoy the party so it will be pointless.	65%

| 3 | Going to bed very late (later than I would have done if I did not have tinnitus) | Unless I am very tired, I will be wide awake listening to my tinnitus. This will make me panicky and uncomfortable. I will not be able to fall asleep for hours. | 99% |
| 4 | I avoid using my hearing aids | Hearing aids will make my tinnitus worse. I will not be able to cope if my tinnitus gets worse. | 85% |

Your menu should have about five to ten items. Try to include a diverse range of items, representative of various aspects of your life that are affected by tinnitus-related avoidance behaviours. You do not need to list every single behaviour, but try to include different types of behaviours. For example, you may use background noise when reading, writing and working on your computer. Provided that you have written down your behaviour of listening to background music in the fear of inability to concentrate due to tinnitus, there is no need to list every single activity (reading, writing, working on your computer). The exposure menu for tinnitus worksheet covers avoidance behaviours while concentrating, trying to sleep, socialising and so on. Try to be open minded and include your worst fears, even if you do not feel that you can face them right now. This can help you to create the bigger picture and highlight the possibilities for improvement in the future.

Dropping avoidance behaviours can be a difficult and stress-producing process, and sometimes it may make you feel that the treatment is worse than the symptoms. This is why it is important to do these preparations. It is important to realise that at this stage you do not need to drop the avoidance behaviours. We are at the planning stage. In the next chapter you will learn more about exactly how to implement procedures to drop avoidance behaviours, as part of your self-help tinnitus management programme. The exposure menu opposite can help you to identify avoidance behaviours and to rate them in terms of how difficult they are to stop. The exposure menu in pages 142–143 was an example. The blank menu in the next page is for you to fill in.

Exposure Menu for Tinnitus worksheet

Exposure Menu for Tinnitus			
Item	Behaviour	What is the fear leading to this behaviour?	How difficult is it for me to stop this behaviour? *Rate the difficulty from 0% 'not difficult at all' to 100% 'impossible'.*
1			
2			
3			
4			

5			
6			
7			
8			
9			
10			

When planning to tackle avoidance behaviours, it can be useful to think of strategies that we might use when we are bothered by tinnitus and when avoidance behaviours are not possible. Based on our clinical experience, approximately a quarter of people with distressing tinnitus use such strategies. These strategies are related to, but different from, avoidance behaviours. The strategies are sometimes used to help alleviate distress or anxiety caused by tinnitus when avoidance techniques are not possible or are impractical. The manner in which such strategies are used is often similar to performing rituals. One class of rituals is known as 'mini-rituals'. These are acts that the person performs in response to anxiety, and they are performed especially by people who experience anxiety associated with obsessive compulsive disorder. For example, a person might try to think some 'good thoughts' over and over again to keep themselves busy, drink a special cup of green tea or seek reassurance from others. Although we may believe that these can help to reduce our anxiety, they can eliminate the effect of our practice of exposure. The whole point of getting rid of avoidance behaviours is to learn that it is possible to tolerate tinnitus and carry out our day-to-day tasks and have a satisfying life even if we hear tinnitus. But if we use such rituals, then this will prevent us from learning that our fears are unfounded. Moreover, rituals usually do not work, and their use may simply make us feel more disappointed. The more annoyed and disappointed we get, the more our brain focuses on the tinnitus. This is the very outcome that we were trying to avoid. The first step in dealing with this is to create a list of rituals that we might adopt when we are bothered by tinnitus. This is called the Rituals Menu for Tinnitus (RMT). The worksheet opposite is an example that includes some typical tinnitus-related rituals. You may use the RMT to write about your own personal experiences with tinnitus.

List up to eight rituals under the second column. Try to be open-minded and list a diverse range of rituals. In the third column, you need to write about your reasons for each ritual. Ask yourself what would happen if you did not do this. In the last column you need to rate how difficult it would be for you if you dropped that particular ritual. You need to rate the anticipated difficulty from 0 per cent 'not difficult at all' to 100 per cent 'extreme difficulty'.

The first RMT is an example. The second is a blank menu for you to fill in.

Example of a Rituals Menu for Tinnitus (RMT) worksheet

Rituals Menu for Tinnitus			
Item	Ritual	What is the fear leading to this ritual?	How difficult is it for me to stop this ritual? *Rate the difficulty from 0% 'not difficult at all' to 100% 'impossible'.*
1	I rush certain activities.	I will not be able to cope. I will not be able to stop thinking about my tinnitus and to focus on the task at hand.	70%
2	I think of some 'good thoughts' over and over again.	The negative thoughts about tinnitus are worse than the tinnitus itself. If I do not push them out of my mind, I will not be able to function.	60%

3	I listen to a mobile phone app or white noise to take the edge off my tinnitus.	I can only engage in conversations with others if I dampen down the tinnitus.	55%
4	I try to relax using deep breathing.	If I don't relax, I will be overwhelmed by tinnitus.	50%
5	I search the Internet for a cure despite knowing the unreliability of many claims on various websites.	If I don't look for a cure then I am not doing anything and that can't be right.	30%
6	I try to keep myself busy.	I will notice the tinnitus more if my mind is not distracted.	80%
7	I seek reassurance over and over again despite already knowing what the answer will be.	I can only believe that tinnitus is not life threatening if my doctor confirms this every time that I ask them.	45%

Rituals Menu for Tinnitus worksheet

Rituals Menu for Tinnitus			
Item	Ritual	What is the fear leading to this ritual?	How difficult is it for me to stop this ritual? *Rate the difficulty from 0% 'not difficult at all' to 100% 'impossible'.*
1			
2			
3			

4		
5		
6		
7		
8		

Dropping rituals can be difficult, since we may think that they are beyond our control, and we may feel very anxious if we try to stop them. This is just the planning stage, and we will discuss the practical implications and methods in Step 7. The next item on the agenda in Step 4 is to learn when CBT should actually be used.

Recognising when to do CBT

Although tinnitus may be present all the time, it may not cause distress or interrupt our activities at all times. We only need to use CBT skills when tinnitus is bothering us (when it is interrupting our activities or affecting our mood) or when we notice changes in our behaviours so as to avoid activities during which we think tinnitus will bother us.

Examples of tinnitus bothering us are:

- Being distracted by tinnitus when reading a book or newspaper

- Being unable to relax and rest when hearing tinnitus

- Having to listen to background music in order to mask tinnitus so we can concentrate on our work

For these examples, CBT skills can be used. As a general rule, CBT skills for tinnitus can be applied whenever tinnitus is the cause of disturbance in our activities or when tinnitus makes us feel anxious, depressed or worried. If we hear tinnitus but it does not affect us, we may not need to use CBT skills at that time.

Examples of tinnitus not bothering you are as follows:

- You hear tinnitus but you can carry out your day-to-day tasks as well as if you didn't have tinnitus

- You hear tinnitus but fall asleep within twenty minutes of going to bed

- You hear tinnitus, but you can still enjoy a TV programme

Of course, for all the above examples it would better if we didn't have tinnitus. However, CBT cannot help us with that. CBT can help us to minimise the effect of tinnitus on us. CBT is not needed when tinnitus does not significantly affect our emotions or behaviours. In fact, hearing tinnitus in such situations sends a message to our brain saying *Look! I can perform this activity even though I am hearing tinnitus.* Therefore, tinnitus loses its significance, which in turn makes it possible for it to fade away into the background.

The key point is to use CBT skills for tinnitus management when the tinnitus is causing some problems (affecting what we are doing or how we feel). However, there may also be times when the direction of causation is reversed (when how we feel and what we do affects our tinnitus).

Some examples of this reversed causation are:

- Loud noises make our tinnitus worse

- Our tinnitus gets louder when we are under stress

- Every time we have a panic attack, our tinnitus changes pitch

In these situations, we might not need to use the CBT skills, provided that the tinnitus is not affecting how we feel or what we do. Instead, noticing these patterns may help us to better understand our tinnitus. We will learn that tinnitus can go up and down but that doesn't mean that it has got worse or that it will stay that way.

> When should we apply CBT skills for tinnitus?
> Whenever it is affecting what we are doing or how we feel.

CBT is not designed to stop changes in tinnitus that might be caused by things such as loud noises or stress. When our tinnitus has changed for any reason, it either affects us or it does not. If it affects us, then CBT can minimise this. So the key point is to consider the impact of tinnitus on us.

To enhance your understanding of when to use CBT skills, use the worksheet overleaf. Choose the scenarios in which you need to use CBT for tinnitus management.

Scenario	Should I use CBT skills for tinnitus?
Loud noises make my tinnitus worse.	Yes/No
I hear tinnitus but I can carry out my day-to-day tasks as well as if I did not have tinnitus.	Yes/No
I can't concentrate on my work due to hearing tinnitus.	Yes/No
My tinnitus sounds louder when I am under stress.	Yes/No
I fall asleep within twenty minutes even though I hear my tinnitus.	Yes/No
I hear tinnitus but I can still enjoy a TV programme.	Yes/No
My tinnitus distracts me from reading a book or newspaper.	Yes/No
I am unable to relax and rest when hearing my tinnitus.	Yes/No
Every time I have a panic attack, my tinnitus changes pitch.	Yes/No

To sum up, a preliminary CBT skill is to know when to use CBT. CBT for tinnitus is only applicable if tinnitus interrupts our activities or affects our mood. In future chapters we discuss more tools that we can use to enhance our skill of knowing when to use CBT.

The correct answers for the scenarios in the worksheet are:

Loud noises make my tinnitus worse.	No
I hear tinnitus but I can carry out my day-to-day tasks as well as if I did not have tinnitus.	No
I can't concentrate on my work due to hearing tinnitus.	Yes
My tinnitus sounds louder when I am under stress.	No
I fall asleep within twenty minutes even though I hear my tinnitus.	No
I hear tinnitus but I can still enjoy a TV programme.	No
My tinnitus distracts me from reading a book or newspaper	Yes
I am unable to relax and rest when hearing my tinnitus.	Yes
Every time I have a panic attack, my tinnitus changes pitch.	No

Step 5. Ready for the Real Thing?

In this section we introduce a method of therapeutic assessment that sets out the direction for the therapy, building on the progress that we have already made in understanding tinnitus and identifying when and for what therapy is needed. The method was developed using the principles of motivational interviewing and through reflecting on the clinical experience of supporting thousands of patients with tinnitus over the past ten years. The method is entitled 4C because it explores 4 aspects of our Confidence in managing tinnitus.

The 4C method sets out to evaluate and simultaneously enhance our confidence in managing tinnitus by encouraging us to think about four different aspects of tinnitus management, as listed below:

- How confident are you that you are able to carry out your day-to-day tasks, even with tinnitus?

- How confident are you that you are able to rest and relax, even with tinnitus?

- How confident are you that you can enjoy your life fully, even with tinnitus?

- How confident are you that you can do all the above without using any avoidance behaviour?

On the questionnaire overleaf read the questions carefully and for each question choose a number that describes best your current level of confidence. You should choose a number from 0 to 10. 0 means that you are 'Not confident at all' in managing in the particular scenario described in the question because of having tinnitus, while 10 means that you are 'Very confident'.

4c Tinnitus Management Questionnaire

For each question, please select one number based on your confidence at the moment.

Q1. How confident are you that you are able to carry out your day-to-day tasks, even with tinnitus?

0	1	2	3	4	5	6	7	8	9	10

Not confident at all   Very confident

Q2. How confident are you that you are able to rest and relax, even with tinnitus?

0	1	2	3	4	5	6	7	8	9	10

Not confident at all   Very confident

Q3. How confident are you that you can enjoy your life fully, even with tinnitus?

0	1	2	3	4	5	6	7	8	9	10

Not confident at all   Very confident

Q4. How confident are you that you can do all the above without using any avoidance behaviour?

0	1	2	3	4	5	6	7	8	9	10

Not confident at all   Very confident

To calculate your overall score for the 4C questionnaire, you need to add up your scores for the first three questions (Q1–Q3) and multiply the result by your score for the fourth question (Q4). Then divide the result by three. This final number is your 4C score. For example, if your scores were '2' for Q1, '1' for Q2, '8' for Q3, and '5' for Q4, then your total score would be:

$$\frac{(2+1+8)\times5}{3} = 18.3$$

The highest possible score is 100, so the total score can be regarded as a percentage. Hence, for the example responses to this questionnaire, the total score for tinnitus management is 18 per cent.

4C scores between 57 per cent and 100 per cent mean that you have a high level of confidence in managing your tinnitus. Scores between 52 per cent and 57 per cent mean that you are fairly confident, scores between 37 per cent and 52 per cent mean that you are slightly confident and scores between 0 and 37 per cent mean that you have low confidence.

If in doubt you can use the online questionnaire, which automatically calculates your score: https://hashirtinnitusclinic.com/4c-tinnitus-management-questionnaire/

> CBT helps us to become more **CONFIDENT** in our day-to-day activities and in our ability to rest, relax and enjoying our life fully, even with tinnitus. More importantly, CBT provides us with the opportunity to become **CONFIDENT** that we can do all these without using any avoidance behaviour.

Now that you have calculated your total 4C score, what is the scope for positive changes to your current tinnitus management skills? Is your 4C score 100 per cent? If not, what can help you to improve it? Use the space below to write down your answer.

To improve my tinnitus management skills I will . . .

_____

_____

_____

In this section, further questions are asked about what you think can help you to move forward and become more confident in managing your tinnitus, based on your answers to each of the 4C questions. It is very important to give these some thought before moving on to the next section. Step 5 is a vital stage. If we are not yet ready, Step 5 can help us to develop readiness. If we are ready, Step 5 can help us to become more confident and committed to the therapy programme. As the Chinese philosopher Confucius (551–479 BC) said, 'In all things success depends on previous preparation, and without such previous preparation there is sure to be failure.'

For the question asking 'How confident are you that you can complete your day-to-day tasks, even with tinnitus', what number did you give? _____

If you gave yourself 0, use the space below to write down your thoughts on why you gave yourself 0.

If you did not give yourself 0, use the space below to write down your thoughts on why you did not give yourself 0.

_____

_____

_____

_____

_____

Here is an example of an answer for a person who rated themselves 6/10:

> I gave myself 6 not 0 because I have had tinnitus for several months and although it annoys me a lot, I am able to do my day-to-day tasks reasonably OK for at least half of the time. 0 would mean that I cannot do anything, which is not true. I can complete my day-to-day tasks most of the time, although it costs me a lot of energy.

Now think what could help you to move to a higher number (unless you gave yourself 10 out of 10)? What would you need to do differently to become confident enough to give yourself a score of 10 out of 10 for your confidence in completing your day-to-day tasks, even with tinnitus? Use the space below to write down your ideas about what might help you to move to a higher number on this question:

_____

_____

_____

_____

_____

Here is an example of an answer for a person who rated themselves 6/10:

I can move to a higher number than 6 if I stop asking myself how this could happen. I must stop hoping things will go back to what they were before, just like that. I must stop worrying about tinnitus and how it will affect my relationship with my wife and family and work. I think my tinnitus is caused by stress, so I try to avoid stress, but maybe that is wrong. Maybe I should live my life as before but take much more time for relaxing and accept that things can go wrong (I realise that I cannot foresee every possible problem that might occur). Now I am busy with tinnitus the whole day because I cannot accept it, but I know in my heart of hearts that there is no cure. I must learn to accept my tinnitus, but so far I have not been able to do it. I need to learn how to accept my tinnitus.

For the question asking 'How confident are you that you are able to rest and relax, even with tinnitus', what number did you give? _____

If you gave yourself 0, use the space below to write down your thoughts on why you gave yourself 0.

If you did not give yourself 0, then use the space below to write down your thoughts on why you did not give yourself 0.

_____

_____

_____

_____

_____

Here is an example of an answer for a person who rated themselves 3/10:

I gave myself 3 not 0 because 0 means no sleep. I have problems sleeping, but I can still sleep sometimes. I use a relaxing noise app, which sometimes helps. I can sometimes sit and have a cup of tea while the noise is bothering me, but I can't say I'm ever fully relaxed while I hear the sounds. To my mind the tinnitus will never sound normal to me.

Now think what could help you to move to a higher number (unless you gave yourself 10 out of 10)? What would you need to do differently to become confident enough to give yourself a score of 10 out of 10 for your confidence that you can rest and relax, even with tinnitus? Use the space below to write down your ideas about what might help you to move to a higher number on this question:

_____

_____

_____

_____

_____

Here is an example of an answer for a person who rated themselves 3/10:

To move to a higher number than 3, I would need to be at peace with hearing the noise in quiet environments, no matter what the noise is like, by putting it into the background. To do this differently my whole mental approach would have to change and become more positive. I need to believe that I can cope with the fluctuations in my tinnitus. I would also like to start each day in a more positive way and break all negative associations with the sound I hear.

For the question asking 'How confident are you that you can enjoy your life fully, even with tinnitus' what number did you give? _____

If you gave yourself 0, use the space below to write down your thoughts on why you gave yourself 0.

If you did not give yourself 0, use the space below to write down your thoughts on why you didn't give yourself 0.

_____

_____

_____

_____

_____

Here is an example of an answer for a person who rated themselves 4/10:

> I gave myself 4 not 0 because I can still run, I
> can walk, play tennis, enjoy my food and watch
> a film.

Now think what could help you to move to a higher number (unless you gave yourself 10 out of 10). What would you need to do differently to become confident enough to give yourself a score of 10 out of 10 for your confidence that you can enjoy your life even with tinnitus? Use the space below to write down your ideas about what might help you to move to a higher number on this question:

_____

_____

_____

_____

_____

Here is an example of an answer for a person who rated themselves 4/10:

> In order to move to a higher number than 4,
> I would need to be able to accept it first thing in
> the morning when I hear it and not care and

think of other things. I need to be able to start fully focusing on my life without dwelling on the noises I hear.

The ultimate goal of tinnitus management based on CBT is to enable you to lead a normal satisfying life without having to be dependent on any avoidance behaviour. For the question asking 'How confident are you that you can do all the above without using avoidance behaviours' what number did you give? _____

If you gave yourself 0, use the space below to write down your thoughts on why you gave yourself 0.

If you did not give yourself 0, use the space below to write down your thoughts on why you didn't give yourself 0.

_____

_____

_____

_____

_____

Here is an example of an answer for a person who rated themselves 5/10:

I gave myself 5 not 0 because I am able to carry out household tasks fine and do cleaning and tidying. I do not need to use background noise during the day. There are also some nights when I can fall asleep without remembering to turn my noise app on.

Now think what could help you to move to a higher number (unless you gave yourself a 10 out of 10). What would you need to do differently to become confident enough to give yourself a score of 10 out of 10 for your confidence that you can manage your tinnitus without using any avoidance techniques? Use the space below to write down your ideas about what might help you to move to a higher number on this question:

_____

_____

_____

_____

_____

Here is an example of an answer for a person who rated themselves 5/10:

To move to a higher number than 5, I need to try harder to reduce my avoidance. The avoidance techniques I use are staying busy, walking outside, doing the dishes, building model cars and using a noise generator at night. I find it very hard to sit still and I think that I must learn to do this so that I am not so tired all the time. I must learn to relax and accept life and moments as they are and not always try to improve them. I need to be confident that I can deal with my tinnitus and that I do not need to rely on avoidance techniques.

Use the worksheet below to summarise your ideas on how to improve your confidence in managing your tinnitus (ignore any questions where you gave yourself a rating of 10 out of 10):

4C question	Your ideas on how to improve
Confidence in completing day-to-day tasks, even with tinnitus	
Confidence that I can rest and relax, even with tinnitus	
Confidence that I can enjoy a satisfying life, even with tinnitus	
Confidence that I can do all the above without using any avoidance behaviour.	

One aim of this ten-step guide is to help you become more confident in managing your tinnitus. So, if you feel ready to move on to the treatment programme, then carry on reading! If you do not feel ready, go back to Step 3.

PART III

Treatment Plan

This part describes the five steps in the programme of treatment.

Step 6. Customise Your Treatment

This step involves the creation of a customised model for your tinnitus distress. In addition, in this step we will explore various personal and life factors that might have contributed to the reaction that you had to tinnitus in the first place.

Constructing the tinnitus model

Here we use the CBT model that was introduced in Step 3 (see Figure 4) to illustrate the connections between the bodily sensations, emotions, behaviours and thoughts that you may experience due to tinnitus. Use Figure 19 (overleaf) as a blank template to create your own model for describing the cycle of your tinnitus distress. The model begins with your initial reactions to tinnitus. Then you have a chain of thoughts that lead to follow-on reactions. The follow-on reactions lead to further evaluative thoughts, creating the vicious cycle.

Our reactions comprise emotions, bodily sensations and behaviours. The initial reaction is the reaction that we have

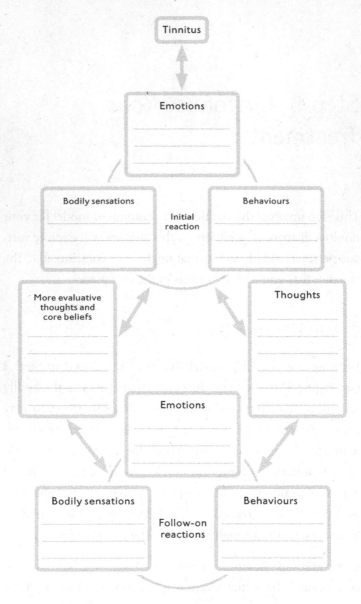

Figure 19: Template for a CBT model.

prior to any thoughts about tinnitus. The follow-on reactions happen as the consequence of our thoughts.

So, what is your initial emotion? You need to identify the first emotion that you feel when you become aware of your tinnitus. Think of times when you were distracted from your tinnitus and then you suddenly started noticing it again. How did your tinnitus make you feel at that very moment, even before you started consciously thinking about it? To use an analogy, imagine that you have gone out for a walk after dinner and you witness a person being brutally beaten. You might immediately feel disgusted, horrified or angry. These are initial emotions that you experience right away, without conscious evaluation. Then you might think about the poor victim and whether they will recover, or you might wonder if the whole area is becoming dangerous. These thoughts can make you feel further upset or worried. So, returning to your CBT model, for the first part of the model you need to write down your initial reactions. An example of an initial reaction for tinnitus is feeling down. Many people say that the moment they wake up and hear tinnitus they immediately feel down.

Here is another example to demonstrate the difference between initial and follow-on emotions as well as initial and follow-on bodily sensations and behaviours. If you are punched on the nose, your initial emotion would probably be shock and the bodily sensation would be pain. You would feel pain before you think about who punched you or why. Your initial behaviours would probably be to close your eyes and cry out. You would probably then have thoughts such as *That was not fair* or *I may be punched again* and you would develop follow-on reactions such as anger (follow-on emotion), an adrenaline rush and increased heartbeat (follow-on bodily sensations) and retaliating or running away (follow-on behaviours). Tinnitus-related initial bodily sensations could be feeling that your ears are blocked or that your own voice sounds strange or distorted. Initial behaviours could be rubbing your ears or avoiding talking. And, as we have already said, an example of an initial emotion for tinnitus is feeling down.

For the thoughts section, list what goes through your mind when your tinnitus bothers you. These are similar to the thoughts that you have explored in Step 4. For example, *I cannot sleep*, *I cannot fix this*, *My life is ruined*, and *I must avoid silence*.

To find out your follow-on reaction, you need to ask what you feel or do when you think of the above-mentioned thoughts. For example, thinking that *I cannot sleep* may make you feel anxious. So, anxiety would be your follow-on emotion. Thinking that *I must avoid silence* can lead to the use of background noise for distraction. This will be your follow-on behaviour. The anxiety and stress caused by your thoughts could also make you feel tense, and the tension may cause headaches. So, feeling tense or having headaches would be your follow-on bodily sensations.

The final stage of the model involves identifying further thoughts and core beliefs. Ask yourself what it means to you that you are experiencing all these emotions, bodily sensations, behaviours and thoughts. What do these tell you about you, the future and life in general? Perhaps you think that they mean that you cannot cope or that you are failing, and the future is bleak, or life is unfair. Write down your deepest fears in this section of the model. You don't need to fully elaborate on these at this stage. We will talk about core beliefs in Step 8.

Now that you have put all of the information in the model, think about which parts of this vicious cycle can be changed or modified (tinnitus, emotions, thoughts, behaviours and bodily sensations).

In order to undertake CBT for tinnitus management, we first need to recognise the right time to use CBT. Secondly, we need to identify the negative thoughts elicited by tinnitus at the moment that we are bothered by it. Thirdly, we need to substitute the negative thoughts with counter-statements for those thoughts. In this chapter, we discuss various techniques and exercises that can help us to achieve these skills. But before moving on to learning techniques for changing our thoughts, it is useful to think back and to try to explore why we developed these thoughts in the first place. The next section is devoted to helping you to understand the root cause of your reaction to tinnitus.

Identifying the root causes of your reaction to tinnitus

When people develop tinnitus, it is very common for them to think about what might have triggered it. When they see a doctor, they often ask what might have caused their tinnitus. However, it is rare that people ask themselves why they reacted to tinnitus in the way that they did. We don't ask ourselves why tinnitus made us feel scared when it started. Perhaps we believe that our reaction to tinnitus is beyond our control. We may think *How can I possibly feel happy hearing this noise screaming in my ears all the time?* or *Because of my tinnitus I am not able to concentrate. I cannot do my work and be successful, and that's reality.* We may think it is realistic to feel anxious if we have tinnitus, which is a condition with no known cure and completely out of our control.

Our psychological reaction to tinnitus is influenced by external events, past experiences, our general health and well-being, and of course our personality. For example, if we have a stressful day at work, we will be more likely to think that we will not be able to cope with our tinnitus. Excessive stress at work might put a strain on our ability to cope. If a family member or a close friend struggled to cope with tinnitus and it ruined their life, this increases the likelihood that we will think that if our tinnitus gets worse we won't be able to manage it. If we have experienced poor health, or have a less than ideal socioeconomic situation, or if we suffer from depression, it is more likely for us to think *I just can't help feeling helpless due to tinnitus.* If we are the type of person who worries a great deal, this makes it more likely that we will develop negative thoughts about our tinnitus and its impact on our life.

For effective management of tinnitus using CBT, it is important to try to understand the factors that might have contributed to our reaction to tinnitus. The aim of CBT is not to undo what has caused our tinnitus, but to modify our reaction to it. Therefore, in the context of CBT, exploration of what might have caused our tinnitus is not as useful as exploring the underlying processes leading to our reactions to the tinnitus. The Tinnitus Reaction Source (TRS) worksheet can be helpful in exploring the root causes of your reactions to tinnitus. In the first column you need to describe the effect of tinnitus on your mood and behaviours when you initially developed tinnitus or when it significantly bothered you more recently. Did it make you feel anxious, panicky or depressed, and did you develop certain avoidance and ritualist behaviours, for example? In the second column there is a list of questions about various factors that might have contributed to your reaction to tinnitus. You may use the third column to write down your answers. A few examples are given on the next two pages. Not all these questions may apply to you, but some of them probably will.

TRS worksheet example

In this example the emotional reaction to tinnitus was *anxiety*.

My reaction to tinnitus	Questions to ask myself	Answers
When I developed tinnitus, I felt very anxious. I could not stay in quiet rooms and had to make myself busy all the time.	Was there a stress-producing life event that might have predisposed me to react in this way or that contributed to the way that I reacted to my tinnitus when I developed it?	When my tinnitus started, I had a new job, and I was trying to learn a lot of new things.
	How have people who are close to me, or were close to me in the past, coped with problems similar to tinnitus?	My uncle had tinnitus and he said it was the worst thing that happened to him, despite experiencing lots of other health issues.
	What is my personality type? Am I a worrier, a perfectionist?	I am a perfectionist.

	How was my general health and well-being?	I was fit and healthy.
	Was I experiencing anxiety or depression prior to or at same time as my tinnitus started?	No, my mental health was absolutely OK before my tinnitus started. I did have stress due to my new job, but nothing that I could not take.

In the above example, the individual did not seem to have any prior history of mental health problems and he was generally fit and healthy. It is possible that his ability to cope was under pressure due to his new job. Changing job and moving house are among the most stress-producing life events. Work-related stress combined with memories of his uncle struggling to cope with tinnitus probably influenced the thoughts that were evoked by his tinnitus; these thoughts contributed to his anxiety. For example, he might have thought: *It is my fault that I have developed tinnitus, I shouldn't have taken this new job, I will not be able to thrive in my new role due to my tinnitus, Just like my uncle, I cannot cope* and *I will end up feeling disabled by tinnitus*. His anxiety and avoidance behaviours might have been heightened as a result of certain thoughts originating from his perfectionist personality, for example *I am not normal, I cannot concentrate on my work due to tinnitus, I will make a lot of errors, this is not acceptable, I am failing.*

> Our reaction to tinnitus is influenced by external events, past life experiences, our general health and well-being, and our personality. But these do not directly cause our reaction. They cause our reaction by creating a certain pattern of thoughts. This ten-step guide helps us to learn how to modify our thoughts, hence modifying our reaction to tinnitus.

Filling in the TRS can help us to understand the reasons behind the way that we reacted to tinnitus in the first place. Sometimes we may feel unsure about why we reacted in the way that we did. We may also feel disappointed and blame ourselves for being distressed by tinnitus. We may think that there are many people in much worse conditions in the world and that it is not right for us to make a big deal out of this. We may feel that our adverse reaction to tinnitus is unjustifiable and is a sign of weakness or perhaps a punishment of some sort. However, filling in the TRS provides an opportunity to reflect on this rationally by putting our reaction to tinnitus in the bigger context of various personal and life factors. After completing the TRS, we may come to the realisation that our reaction to tinnitus was justified and was a normal human reaction given our background and the circumstances that we were in.

Below is another example of a TRS worksheet. In this example, the emotional reaction to tinnitus was feeling *hopeless*.

My reaction to tinnitus	Questions to ask myself	Answers
I felt hopeless. I reduced talking with my family and friends over the phone in the fear that noises from the telephone would make my tinnitus worse.	Was there a stress-producing life event that might have predisposed me to react in this way or that contributed to the way that I reacted to my tinnitus when I developed it?	COVID-19 lock down
	How have people who are close to me, or were close to me in the past, coped with problems similar to tinnitus?	My mum had dementia and had a very sad life.
	What is my personality type? Am I a worrier, a perfectionist . . .?	I am a 'glass-half-empty' type person. I think more of bad things most of the time.

	How was my general health and wellbeing?	No other health issues.
	Was I experiencing anxiety or depression prior to or at same time as when my tinnitus started?	I have depression and have been taking anti-depressants to manage it for many years.

In the above example, the individual was fit and healthy and only the COVID-19 pandemic was a life event that might have influenced her reaction to tinnitus. A history of depression and a personality type consistent with pessimism could increase the likelihood of developing negative thoughts. Examples of such thoughts are *Life is unfair*, *There is no hope*, *Because of tinnitus I will be unable to be normal and will end up being isolated and sad*. Memories of how dementia affected her mum could also have heightened the feeling of hopelessness by developing thoughts such as *I will end up like my mum, lonely and sad* and *I am worthless, and no one cares*.

Use the TRS worksheet to explore possible root causes of your reaction to tinnitus.

TRS worksheet

My reaction to tinnitus	Questions to ask myself	Answers
	Was there a stress-producing life event that might have predisposed me to react in this way or that contributed to the way that I reacted to my tinnitus when I developed it?	
	How have people who are close to me, or were close to me in the past, coped with problems similar to tinnitus?	

	What is my personality type? Am I a worrier, a perfectionist . . .?	
	How was my general health and wellbeing?	
	Was I experiencing anxiety or depression prior to or at same time as my tinnitus started?	

Gaining a better understanding of the possible factors influencing the reaction to tinnitus can help to explain why people react differently. It is worth mentioning that life events, facts of life and our personality characteristics do not directly cause our reaction to tinnitus. Their possible effect is indirect and it is through the generation of certain patterns of thoughts that we develop in reaction to our tinnitus. Hence, we should not get side-tracked by paying too much attention to the factors that might have contributed to our reaction to tinnitus, as they usually can't be changed anyway. For example, it can be difficult or impossible to change our personality or to remove memories of past events. In fact, even trying to make changes to life factors can often be counterproductive in the management of tinnitus. For example, if we try to change our job to one with less stress, this does not guarantee that we won't be stressed in the new job, and the very process of changing jobs is stressful.

Moreover, the more changes we make in our life because of tinnitus, the more important the tinnitus becomes, the very outcome that we are trying to avoid. The solution lies in identifying and modifying the thoughts generated by the tinnitus. If the negative thoughts are modified, regardless of their source, our reaction to tinnitus will also be modified. In Steps 3 and 4, we practised how to identify our thoughts and how to pinpoint the key troublesome thoughts, the *hot* thoughts. In Step 6, so far, we have learned about our own CBT model and the factors that could have contributed to our reaction to tinnitus. In the next part of Step 6, we will learn more about the characteristics of the negative thoughts generated by tinnitus.

How can I change my thoughts about tinnitus? Introducing automatic thoughts

So far in this book, we have talked about thoughts in general. We also talked about *hot* thoughts, which are the thoughts that bother us the most. Now it is time to introduce the concept of 'automatic thoughts'. No need to get panicky! They are still just thoughts and most of the thoughts that we have identified in the previous chapters are in fact automatic thoughts. But it is interesting to learn more about them because they are linked directly to our emotional reactions. Automatic thoughts arise spontaneously, without any deliberate reasoning, and flow rapidly through our minds with little awareness as to why they arise; they don't seem to be under our direct control, in that we can't simply decide which thoughts should appear in a given scenario.

As described by Professor Judith Beck, when we are reading a book, part of our mind is processing the information and integrating the information with our background knowledge on the subject. This reflects our more obvious rational thinking. At the same time, at another level we may have some quick evaluative automatic thoughts. These are spontaneous and not a result of deliberation or reasoning. We may barely be aware of them while reading. For example, while reading this book, a quick thought could be *What if I cannot learn CBT and utilise it for my tinnitus? I will never be able to deal with my tinnitus. No one can help me in this matter. This will ruin my life.* We are more likely to be aware of the emotions and behaviours related to these automatic thoughts than the thoughts themselves. For example, we may feel anxious or down when reading this book or we may feel hopeless and abandon reading the book altogether.

It does not come to us naturally to notice, challenge or modify our automatic thoughts, but this is required by CBT. The idea that it is difficult to control our automatic thoughts is not new. Over 800 years ago, Rumi said: 'Your thinking is like a horse rider, and you are the horse. It drives you in every direction under its bitter control'. What we usually do notice is the effect that automatic thoughts have on our mood and behaviour. We tend to link various life events (recall A in the ABC model, page 95) to our emotional reactions (recall C in the ABC model) to them. For example, we may have noticed that someone behaved in a certain way or said something inappropriate (a life event), and this made us feel angry or upset (our emotional reaction). We might not necessarily be aware of the automatic thoughts (recall B in the ABC model) about that behaviour that made us feel angry or upset.

> In ABC model, 'A' represents Activating events or situations, 'B' represents Beliefs or underlying thoughts, and 'C' represents the Consequences or reactions, which may be emotional, behavioural or physiological.

In CBT, we have to develop the skill of doing something that does not come naturally to us. We need to be able to become explicitly aware of our automatic thoughts, challenge them and modify them. Although these skills do not come to us naturally, it is possible to learn them. There are lots of skills that do not come to us naturally. It does not come to us naturally to play the violin or to swim. But taking lessons and practising can help us to gain these skills. The same applies to learning CBT, and it takes time. We can learn CBT by understanding its theoretical underpinnings and by practising the skills that it requires. Although it may seem impossible to control your reaction to tinnitus, CBT says that you can, and that you do this partly by modifying your automatic thoughts!

What you will learn in Step 6 is that even though you may be convinced that your thoughts are true and valid, there can be a lot of errors in them. And you are not alone in this! Thought errors, also known as thought distortions, are common in all human beings. In fact, thought distortions might have worked well for us in evolutionary terms. Anyone can experience thoughts that they believe are true but that are in fact distorted and unrealistic. Learning that our thoughts can have some errors in them can make us more ready to move towards changing them.

Aaron Beck suggested that human emotional disturbances are related to a number of distortions in automatic thoughts. These range from over-generalisation to all-or-nothing thinking. Note that several of these thought distortions can occur at the same time, and the types of distortions may overlap.

Common thought distortions are listed below:

* All-or-nothing thinking

* Over-generalisation

* Mental filtering (biased thinking)

* Discounting the positive

* Jumping to conclusions

* Exaggeration

* Emotional rather than factual reasoning

* 'Should' statements (statements about how things ought to be)

* Labelling (reducing to an over-simplified form)

* Personalisation and blame

All-or-nothing thinking is thinking in extremes. For example, we may believe that either we are totally successful in managing our tinnitus or we are completely unsuccessful; there are no grey areas. As a real example, when a university student could only concentrate enough to understand 80 per cent of a lecture because of his tinnitus, he told himself that there was no point in attending the class at all. Other examples of all-or-nothing thinking are: *I can no longer have a normal life, I can't be comfortable even in a quiet room, I have blown my life completely by not being careful enough with loud noises, I cannot trust doctors anymore, What is the point of booking a holiday if I won't be able to enjoy it at all?, If I can't enjoy being in silence as much as I used to, it means that I enjoy nothing, I am weak and vulnerable, I am not good enough, No one understands me, I am unlovable, I have nothing to look forward to, Tinnitus is spoiling my appreciation of this music, so there is no point in listening to music at all.*

Over-generalisation is drawing broad conclusions from a limited amount of information. A person with tinnitus had difficulty falling asleep at night. He told himself *I will never be able to have a good night's sleep.* Other examples are: *I will never be able to do any task without being aware of the presence of this ringing, I won't ever enjoy going to a social event, I will not be able to enjoy any leisure activities, I will always be exhausted and stressed, This will always be the first thing I am aware of when I wake up, I will always start the day feeling frustrated, I will never be unaffected by tinnitus, I am stuck with this forever, I will never be able to fall asleep naturally again, It will never be easy to wake up and then fall back asleep with this noise in my ears.*

Mental filtering is a form of biased thinking. We tend to pay attention to evidence that confirms our pre-existing ideas. Information that is consistent with a pre-existing idea is taken as proof that the idea is correct while information that contradicts the idea is ignored as insignificant or regarded as a fluke. For example, a man who believed that he could not enjoy his life due to tinnitus did not remember the occasions when he enjoyed himself despite hearing tinnitus. Rather, he gave greater importance to occasions where he did not enjoy himself due to his tinnitus. This mental filter gave him an unbalanced view about his ability to enjoy life even when hearing tinnitus.

This is a difficult error to tackle, as by its nature the mental filter stops us from seeing the other side of the story. Once an erroneous idea is entrenched, many years of life experiences contrary to that idea will not change it.

Discounting the positive is a tendency to focus on bad experiences rather than good experiences. It takes the joy of life away. For example, if a person sometimes enjoys meals in restaurants and sometimes does not, because their tinnitus bothers them, they mainly remember the times when the tinnitus did affect their enjoyment of the meal. In general, occasions where tinnitus does interfere with the enjoyment of certain activities are focused on. Thoughts focus on the things that tinnitus interrupts, while the times that tinnitus has no impact are not taken into consideration.

Jumping to conclusions can take two forms: mind reading and fortune telling. Mind reading involves making assumptions about what other people are thinking. For example, a man who finds it hard to concentrate at work when he is aware of his tinnitus may think: *Because of my tinnitus I have not been performing well at work and my boss thinks that I am useless.* Fortune telling involves predictions, and as the American author Mark Twain said: *It's difficult to make predictions, especially about the future.* For example, if you know that you have a difficult new task at work coming up, you may tell yourself: *I will not be able to perform this new task because my tinnitus disturbs my concentration.*

Other examples of jumping to conclusions are: *I will not be able to have a stable job, I will not be able to engage properly in this conversation because I'm thinking about my tinnitus, I have to read a sentence many times to absorb it, so I can't read a book, Because of my lack of concentration due to tinnitus, I will not be able to fulfil my potential and do things in life I want to, My tinnitus is going to continue getting worse and become a bigger problem, I will become depressed, I won't be able to sleep properly, I won't be able to function properly, I'm too focused on my tinnitus and that's going to cause it to get louder and not go away, My tinnitus stopped me from sleeping last night, so I will probably be unable to sleep tonight, even though I am very tired, My reputation at work will be destroyed because I did not perform well at work yesterday, I will be excluded, I will be lonely, People won't want to be around me, If I don't control my tinnitus then it will get worse.*

Exaggeration involves over-estimating the negative consequences of a problem. For example, we may think that *Tinnitus has completely ruined my life, Lack of sleep because of my tinnitus has ruined my work, I will never be able to cope with my tinnitus, I will never have peace and quiet, I am a worthless person because of my tinnitus, The rest of my life is going to be spoiled by my tinnitus, I'm kidding myself if I think I can get used to this* or *There is no solution for this.*

Emotional reasoning is thinking based on emotions rather than facts. For example, we may think: *I feel annoyed by my tinnitus, so I will not be able to read a book, I feel horrified because of tinnitus, and this proves that tinnitus is a terrible disease, I feel hopeless and this means that there is no way to cope with my tinnitus, Because loud noises frighten me, they will make my tinnitus worse and I will be exhausted and get a headache, I feel very angry and stressed by my tinnitus, which means that it overpowers me, I feel hopeless, which means there is no hope and tinnitus will stop me from falling asleep.*

'Should' statements are thoughts based on our view of how things ought to be. Dr Albert Ellis famously referred to should statements as 'musturbations'. In his interviews, he said that masturbation is good, but musturbation is not. For example, we may think: *Most people don't have tinnitus, so if I am to have a normal life, I must get rid of my tinnitus. The doctors must be able to cure this.* Another example is: *I shouldn't have gone to this noisy place because I know that noise always makes my tinnitus worse.* Or we may think: *People are inconsiderate; they shouldn't make such loud noises.* Should statements directed at ourselves often lead to guilt and sadness, while if they are directed at others they may lead to anger, hostility and frustration. Other examples of should statements are: *I shouldn't have these thoughts in my mind, but I can't get rid of them, so I am inadequate* and *I should be able to deal with tinnitus as many other people have to deal with much bigger problems. I am letting myself and others down.*

Labelling is a form of all-or-nothing thinking. The complexities of human thoughts, feelings and emotions are reduced to an oversimplified form. For example, if we make a mistake, instead of thinking how we can do better we may label ourselves as a loser and give up. Labelling doesn't give us any direction for improvement, and it contributes to a feeling of hopelessness.

Personalisation and blame are types of thought distortions whereby negative events are attributed to ourselves instead of to the context or circumstances. For example, someone who developed tinnitus after attending a rock concert may think: *It is my own fault, I should not have gone to that noisy concert,* instead of thinking: *Tinnitus can happen to anyone, and I could not have known that I would get tinnitus as a result of the noisy concert. I need to think about how I can move forward and get on with my life.*

CBT is not intended to make us happy all the time. That would not be realistic. The aim is to identify and modify the negative thoughts that are based on inherent errors of judgement. In other words, the aim of CBT is to change unrealistic and unhelpful thoughts to more realistic ones.

Next, we talk about some more examples of common thought distortions with regard to tinnitus.

One common thought is *Hearing tinnitus always makes me feel tired*. The use of 'always' in this thought is a sign of over-generalisation. We may feel tired due to tinnitus sometimes, or even frequently, but not always. Another probable thought distortion here is the mental filter. This filter makes us focus on the times when we feel tired (perhaps due to tinnitus). Any time that we are tired and hear our tinnitus will be taken as proof of the validity of this thought. However, we don't take notice of the times when we do not feel tired, despite the permanent and continuous nature of our tinnitus. Such thought distortions enhance negative thoughts about tinnitus, using biased and erroneous information.

Another common thought is: *Tinnitus invades every aspect of my life. This makes me useless*. Use of 'every' in this thought is a sign of over-generalisation. Again, another distortion is the mental filter. This filter makes us focus on the aspects of our life that have been adversely affected by tinnitus. Finally, *This makes me useless* is an example of labelling. We label ourselves as useless instead of reviewing what we can and cannot achieve. Other examples of labelling are calling ourselves a fool, a failure or a loser. These labels lead to anger, depressed mood and low self-esteem. Labelling can also be connected to other thought distortions. It can be a form of all-or-nothing thinking, where we, as complex human beings, are taken out of context and reduced to one characteristic (e.g. if I cannot always concentrate, then I am useless). Labels are also likely to be over-generalised, since we assume that we are always like this. This is irrational because we are much more complex than that.

The Tinnitus-Related Thought Distortions (TRTD) worksheet can be used to practise the skill of identifying your tinnitus-related thought distortions. When filling in the TRTD worksheet, you can use the events and thoughts from your THT worksheet (page 128) in which you identified your *hot* thoughts. In the third column, write down the distortions that you can identify in your thoughts.

Tinnitus–Related Thought Distortions (TRTD) worksheet example

Event	Thoughts	Distortions
Example. It is Tuesday 5 pm I am watching TV and my tinnitus is interfering with my enjoyment.	'Damn this noise! This is awful! I cannot enjoy watching TV any-more. I will never be able to enjoy my life.'	Magnification: I was still able to follow the programme and to get some enjoyment out of it. Of course, it would be much better if I didn't have tinnitus. but I still enjoyed watching. Future telling: How do I know that I will not be able to enjoy TV in the future? All or nothing thinking: If I can't enjoy certain things as well as I used to, this does not mean that I will enjoy nothing.

The aim of this exercise is not to change our thoughts, but to practise identifying distortions or biases in our tinnitus-related negative thoughts. This exercise is like digging a tunnel under the wall of tinnitus-related thoughts. It is well known that digging tunnels under walls weakens them, which makes it easier to smash them down. This was a technique used by Assyrian ancient tribes when they were attacking a castle. In Step 8, there will be more practice on changing thoughts and smashing the wall! But before that we need to implement the behaviour changes that we planned for in Step 4. Step 7 teaches us how to systematically tackle our avoidance behaviours and to learn from that.

> Identifying distortions and errors in our thoughts can make us more willing to change them. This is like digging a tunnel under the wall of tinnitus-related negative thoughts, making it easier to smash it down later on.

Step 7. Start to SEL (Stop Avoidance, Expose and Learn)!

In Step 4, we learned about avoidance behaviours and rituals and the negative reinforcement they can cause. One of the main CBT skills is to *Stop* avoidance behaviours and rituals, *Expose* ourselves to our fears, and *Learn* if there is any truth in them.

In Step 7 of this self-help book, we learn about a method that we can use to test our thoughts through changing our behaviours. The acronym SEL is used for this method: 'S' for stopping avoidance, 'E' for expose ourselves to tinnitus, and 'L' to learn from it. The SEL method involves a form of experiment that we try for ourselves.

SEL is a seven-day activity, and it has two benefits: (1) it helps us to challenge our tinnitus-related thoughts; and (2) it helps us to improve our tolerance for tinnitus and the negative emotions it may cause.

We may ask how a successful outcome would look after completing SEL. The measure of success in SEL is not a reduction in tinnitus or an improvement in sleep or even a reduction in anxiety. SEL is successful when we can face our fears and learn that the tinnitus-related difficulties and the negative emotions it causes are manageable. SEL prepares us not to be afraid of tinnitus. It prepares us for the next step.

You need to use the SEL worksheet on page 206 for this step. In the first column, write down the behaviour and/or ritual that you would like to stop (e.g. listening to the radio while trying to get to sleep). In the second column, list the problems that you expect if you stop the behaviour or ritual listed in the first column. Use the third column to rate the severity of the problems that you expect before the situation has occurred. Expose yourself to the situation (e.g. trying to get to sleep) while avoiding the avoidance behaviour and/or ritual (e.g. keeping the radio off) and use the fourth column to rate the actual level of difficulty that you experienced. Finally write down in the bottom row what you have learned from each SEL experiment. This is just a summary of the SEL process. More detailed instructions on how to SEL are given in the next few pages.

Safety note

Use the SEL worksheet for testing thoughts about usual activities that do not pose any risk of harm to you or others. The SEL should not be used for testing thoughts about the effect of tinnitus on driving, piloting, shooting, working with explosives, surgical operations, working with heavy machinery or any other types of operations that could cause physical harm to you or to people around you. If your key negative thoughts about tinnitus are related to such activities, then you should see a tinnitus specialist/therapist, who can offer comprehensive therapy.

In order to complete the SEL worksheet, please go back to Step 4 and your answers for the worksheets Exposure Menu for Tinnitus (EMT) on page 145 and Rituals Menu for Tinnitus (RMT) on page 149. Use the behaviours/rituals identified in your EMT and RMT for the SEL experiment. You should start the SEL with behaviours that you have rated as less difficult to stop on the EMT and RMT worksheets. The more difficult behaviours are tackled later.

In the first column in the SEL worksheet, write down the behaviour that you would like to stop as well as any associated rituals that you often find yourself doing when that behaviour is not possible. For example, the behaviour to stop could be listening to the radio when going to bed at night, and the rituals could be deep breathing or counting backward when the radio is not available. Note that not everyone has ritualist behaviours. So, if you haven't identified any rituals in your RMT then there is no need to consider them in the SEL. The main point is not to replace the target avoidance behaviour with other avoidance behaviours or rituals.

In the second column, write down your negative thoughts about the difficulties that you fear if you stop the avoidance behaviour. In other words, write down what you think might happen if you stop that particular behaviour. For example, the

The SEL worksheet

What behaviours and/or rituals should I stop?	What problems do I think will occur if I stop the behaviour?	What do I predict the severity of the anticipated problems will be? Rate from 0 to 100% (100% is the most severe). (Record this *before exposure*)	The actual severity of the problems I experienced. Rate from 0 to 100% (100% is the most severe). (Record this *after exposure*)
Behaviour/ritual	Problem number 1	?%	Day 1: ?%
	Problem number 2	?%	?%
	Problem number 3	?%	?%
	Problem number 4	?%	?%

Day 2: ?% ?% ?% ?% ?%	Day 3: ?% ?% ?% ?% ?%	Day 4: ?% ?% ?% ?% ?%	Day 5: ?% ?% ?% ?%

Day 6: ?% ?% ?% ?%	Day 7: ?% ?% ?% ?%	
		What did I learn?

thoughts could be: *My tinnitus will sound louder, I will feel anxious* and *I will not be able to fall asleep*. About three to four thoughts about the problems that you think will occur if you stop the behaviour will be enough.

In the third column, write down the severity of the difficulties that you anticipate you will have if you abandon the behaviour (e.g. it will take me longer to fall asleep if I don't listen to the radio). For each problem in the second column, rate the severity of the anticipated difficulty that it will cause from 0 to 100 per cent (100 per cent is the worst), for example how loud the tinnitus will be, how much anxiety you will experience, and how long it will take you to fall asleep. When you answer these questions, think of the worst scenario that you can imagine.

Then carry out the SEL experiment for one week, for each of the behaviours you wrote down in the first column of the worksheet. For each day, expose yourself to the situation without your usual behaviour/ritual (e.g. try to go to sleep without having the radio on). In the fourth column, record the actual severity of the difficulty that you experienced with regard to each problem that you listed in the second column. If you do this for one week you will probably notice that the actual effect of abandoning the behaviour/ritual is less than you anticipated; the rated difficulty in column four is smaller than the anticipated difficulty in column three. If you practise SEL for several weeks you may also notice that the percentages in the fourth column reduce over time.

It is also possible that the percentages in the fourth column are similar to what you have anticipated or even worse, especially at the start of SEL. It is important to continue with the SEL for several weeks. It is very likely that you will notice a reduction in the scores in the fourth column over time. It is important to ask yourself: *What did I learn from SEL? Were the actual difficulties that I experienced as bad as I anticipated them to be?* Each week, write down what you have learned in the bottom row of the SEL worksheet.

You can move on to SEL for a different behaviour once you no longer are afraid of abandoning a given behaviour. Then you can start to use SEL for a behaviour that is more difficult for you to stop, as identified in Step 4.

> Completing SEL always leads to success. We may learn that our predicted negative thoughts were not realised, in which case we can change them. Alternatively, if the experience was as bad as we anticipated, SEL helps us to improve our tolerance of tinnitus and the negative emotions it may cause.

You may not be able or willing to perform SEL every day for the whole week. This is absolutely OK and normal. You are only human! Sometimes we may not feel like doing something. Sometimes we may feel less motivated or even tired of undertaking a particular activity. Think of it as if you were going to learn how to cycle. Of course, you will learn more quickly if you practise non-stop for a few days. But would that be feasible? You might get tired, fall over, need to rest or have other more important activities. So there is no point in getting disappointed if you need to stop to get some rest. This is essential and we need to factor it in. The same is true for SEL. You need to allow for the fact that on some days you may not want to practise SEL. That is why in our clinics we introduced Did Not Do it (DND) cards, or free passes. So, before starting to practise SEL, you need to think how many DND cards you would like to give to yourself, i.e. days when you are allowed to skip the experiment. Then stick to that.

Let's talk about a patient, John, who completed the SEL worksheet. John had severe difficulties in falling asleep at night due to his tinnitus. He developed a safety-seeking behaviour of listening to podcasts when going to bed at night as a distraction from tinnitus. Although this might have helped him to reduce his awareness of his tinnitus, he was still significantly affected by it and by fears of it getting louder, to the point that he could no longer distract himself from it by listening to podcasts. He was afraid that if his tinnitus got worse he would not be able to fall asleep at night, and that this would lead to tiredness and adversely affect his daily activities. John decided to stop the avoidance behaviour of listening to podcasts at night for his SEL experiment for two weeks. His SEL worksheet is shown on the next page. He anticipated that he would have certain difficulties if he stopped his avoidance behaviour. These were listed in the second column: 'It will take me longer to fall asleep', 'I will feel anxious', 'I will be tired the next day' and 'I will not be able to concentrate on my work the next day'.

John's SEL worksheet before starting exposure

What behaviours and rituals should I stop?	What problems do I think will occur if I stop the behaviour?	What do I predict the severity of the anticipated problems will be? Rate from 0 to 100% (100% is the most severe). (Record this *before* exposure)	The actual severity of the problems I experienced. Rate from 0 to 100% (100% is the most severe). (Record this *after* exposure)
Behaviour/ritual (if applicable) Listening to a podcast when going to bed at night.	Problem number 1: It will take me longer to fall asleep.	100%	Day 1: ?%
	Problem number 2: I will feel anxious.	100%	?%
	Problem number 3: I will be tired the next day.	100%	?%
	Problem number 4: I will not be able to concentrate on my work the next day.	100%	?%

Day 2: ?% ?% ?% ?%	Day 3: ?% ?% ?% ?%	Day 4: ?% ?% ?% ?%	Day 5: ?% ?% ?% ?%

Day 6: ?% ?% ?% ?%	Day 7: ?% ?% ?% ?%	
		What did I learn?

It is best to include a diverse range of anticipated problems in the second column. In John's example, he included problems about his sleep and how he would feel, and then some thoughts about the impact of sleep deprivation on his daytime activities. So - try to think broadly and capture a wide spectrum of anticipated problems. For instance, if you use SEL to stop listening to background noise whilst working, then add thoughts about whether you will be able to do your work as efficiently as you would like (e.g. my efficiency will be reduced), how you will feel (e.g. I will feel disappointed), what others will think of your work (e.g. my boss will think that I am lazy), and the impact that these things might have on your personal life (e.g. having a bad day at work will make it harder to cope with my tinnitus and as a result when I get home I will be snappy with my partner).

The next step was for John to rate the severity of the difficulty he anticipated experiencing in relation to each of his negative thoughts and problems, as listed in column 2. So, for the thought 'It will take me longer to fall asleep' his answer was 100 per cent (the worst possible outcome). He also rated the anticipated anxiety, tiredness and lack of concentration on the next day at the maximum (100 per cent). The table on pages 212–214 shows his SEL worksheet before starting the exposure.

John gave himself three DND cards. Then he stopped using the podcasts at night. He also made sure that he did not replace this behaviour with other avoidance behaviours or rituals. He carried on with SEL for two weeks. He ended up not using his DND cards. Figure 20 shows his ratings for each day.

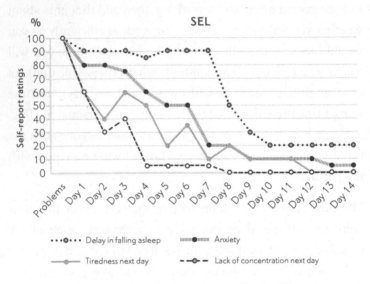

Figure 20: Results of conducting SEL for John.

As shown in Figure 20, the first lesson for John was that the impact of lack of sleep on his tiredness and concentration on the next day was less than predicted. This became apparent to him during the first few days of SEL. This was an important learning outcome, since fear of the impact of lack of sleep on his ability to cope on the next day contributed to his experience of anxiety when going to bed at night. This helped him to modify his negative thought of: *I will not be able to concentrate on my work the next day* to *I will be able to concentrate enough on my tasks despite the lack of sleep.* Changing this negative thought reduced his anxiety and therefore his fear of anxiety. He also realised that he did not feel excessively tired during the day. So, from day 7 his scores for anxiety and impact on the next day were minimal and remained that way. Once his negative predictions about the impact of sleep deprivation and about anxiety proved to be not as bad as he predicted, his ratings for delay in falling asleep improved too.

To sum up, for John to minimise the impact of tinnitus on his sleep he needed to face his fears. Once he stopped his avoidance behaviour, he learned that some of his anticipated difficulties were not as great as he feared and he changed his thoughts as a consequence. Persisting with exposure to his feared scenario made him more confident that he could manage this, which eventually improved his ability to get to sleep. Here is some feedback from John about what helped him to get over his tinnitus. He wrote: '*Since doing my therapy, dealing with tinnitus has just become a simple routine like brushing my teeth or eating dinner. The techniques that I was taught have become second nature to me now and have helped with issues even outside of my tinnitus. Having these skills now has really boosted my confidence in general too. Through realising the fake worries I gave myself and setting small goals, I am where I am now. It takes time but it's worth that time.*'

His post-exposure SEL worksheet for week one is shown on the next page.

John's SEL worksheet for week one

What behaviours and rituals should I stop?	What problems do I think will occur if I stop the behaviour?	What do I predict the severity of the anticipated problems will be? Rate from 0 to 100% (100% is the most severe). (Record this *before exposure*)	The actual severity of the problems I experienced. Rate from 0 to 100% (100% is the most severe). (Record this *after exposure*)
Behaviour/ritual (if applicable) Listening to a podcast when going to bed at night.	Problem number 1: It will take me longer to fall asleep.	100%	Day 1: 90%
	Problem number 2: I will feel anxious.	100%	80%
	Problem number 3: I will be tired the next day.	100%	60%
	Problem number 4: I will not be able to concentrate on my work the next day.	100%	60%

Day 2: 90% 80% 40% 30%	Day 3: 90% 75% 60% 40%	Day 4: 85% 60% 50% 5%	Day 5: 90% 50% 20% 5%

Day 6: 90% 50% 35% 5%			
Day 7: 90% 20% 10% 5%			

What did I learn? I learned that I can fall asleep even with tinnitus. I can concentrate on my tasks most of the time during the day despite the tinnitus and sleep problems.

It is important to take stock of the outcome of the SEL process. The SEL process is intended to help us to find out whether our negative predictions and fears are justified. Most people find that at least some of their predictions do not come true. For example, they could still enjoy certain activities, socialise or carry out their day-to-day tasks despite their tinnitus. Often our negative predictions about the impact of tinnitus on our lives are exaggerated and not a true reflection of reality. We may think that because of tinnitus we can no longer enjoy our life. This very thought can lead to low mood, which in turn makes it difficult for us to enjoy life. But when this thought is broken down into smaller activities and tested with the use of the SEL worksheet, it might become apparent that there are lots of activities that we can enjoy even with tinnitus. This learning outcome can be used to develop rational thoughts, also called counter-statements, that we can use to substitute the irrational thoughts.

We can use our observations during the SEL process to learn a different perspective about our tinnitus and its impact. Make a comparison between the predicted difficulty and the actual difficulty that you recorded in the SEL worksheet. Use this information to develop counter-statements for your negative thoughts. Examples of counter-statements are: 'I can enjoy reading a book most of the time and this makes me feel happy' or 'Although I hear tinnitus and I am still awake, I am resting in my comfortable bed'.

The SEL process is based on exposure and learning from it to help us test the validity of our negative predictions/thoughts about tinnitus and the helpfulness of our responses to these thoughts. Once we have identified helpful ways to respond to tinnitus and our thoughts and beliefs about it, with the help of CBT, any anxiety and negative emotions caused by tinnitus may start to subside, which is also likely to reduce the perception of tinnitus. However, it would be counterproductive to aim to reduce the perception of tinnitus, as this cannot be achieved directly. It is more likely for it to be achieved by changing our emotional response to tinnitus via modifying our tinnitus-related thoughts and behaviours. Our focus should be on learning CBT techniques and modifying our thoughts and behaviours in response to tinnitus. Once we achieve this, an automatic process will kick in whereby our brain reduces the perception of all types of stimuli that are not emotionally significant.

It is understandable for us to wonder whether doing all these SEL experiments will help. It is very natural to be worried about the outcome and to doubt if we will be able to cope. However, all these are simply distractions that you need to ignore. Let us elaborate on this a bit more. Imagine that you have a badly broken arm or leg, and you go to an orthopaedic surgeon who inserts pins to fix the broken limb. At the time of the operation, would you want the surgeon to think how much pain you are experiencing due to the break, whether you will be able to resume a normal life, whether you will be able to engage in sports activities, and so on, or would you want the surgeon to focus on fixing your broken bone, making sure the parts are aligned correctly and that no infection is

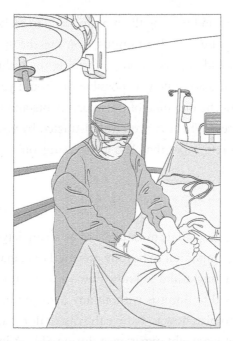

Figure 21: In CBT, **you are the surgeon**! *Like an orthopaedic surgeon who should not get distracted by thoughts about the outcome of the operation and should focus on doing the job properly, you need to focus on using CBT techniques correctly as opposed to ruminating about whether or not your tinnitus will get quieter.*

introduced? Most people say that they would want the surgeon to focus on the technical aspects of the operation and not to be distracted by thoughts about the outcome of the operation or the impact of the broken bone on your future. This is one of the reasons that surgeons do not often operate on members of their own family. If they did, it would be much harder for them not to think of possible consequences of the operation, adding to their stress and making them more likely to make mistakes. Now to practise CBT for tinnitus, you are the surgeon. Yes, you! So, should you focus on performing the techniques and experiments as accurately as possible or should you be ruminating about the outcome of the experiments and their future consequences? Whenever you feel distracted by your thoughts and doubts remember that 'You are the surgeon'.

What if I cannot perform SEL?

Exposure during SEL is most likely to be an anxiety-producing process. It is important to be fully prepared to manage this. For example, we might like to know how to calm ourselves down when exposed to tinnitus without any background noise. We might like to plan how to reduce the discomfort, agitation and sadness that we might experience during SEL. A logical question that you might have is: 'How do I dampen down negative feelings during SEL?' The answer is very counterintuitive. The answer is that 'You don't'. This might surprise you, since based on what you have learned so far in this book the main aim of CBT is to manage your emotional reactions to tinnitus. So how can it be that the advice here is not to try to control your emotions? You are right. The aim of CBT is to manage our emotional reactions to tinnitus, but not too fast!

Let's think about an example to make the point. Boxing is a sport whose key goal is to punch your opponent. But most professional boxers do not rush in using all their strength and throwing their best punches as soon as the match starts. You have to be strategic in using your resources when you are in a boxing match. Perhaps you should first take some punches to warm up and measure up your opponent. Perhaps you should 'mix it up' with them to assess how much they can hurt you. After all, pain is an integral part of boxing, and the combatants expect to feel some pain. Think of the example that was discussed before, 'The Rumble in the Jungle', Muhammad Ali versus George Foreman. Ali did not rush in using all his might and throwing his best punches as soon as the match started. First, he took a lot of punches, which surely must have hurt. Similarly, we can expect to experience annoyance, irritation, sadness and other negative emotions while learning how to manage tinnitus using CBT. In boxing, if we start throwing our best punches as soon as the match starts in the fear of being hurt, then we may become exhausted and lose the match. To improve our chances of winning a boxing match, we need to overcome our fear of the inevitable pain. In boxing it is not possible to perform at our best if we are focused on avoiding pain. Similarly, effective tinnitus management is not possible if we are afraid of having negative and uncomfortable emotions.

So, during SEL we should be prepared to feel negative emotions and uncomfortable experiences. This is consistent with a poem from Rumi, which emphasises the need to face our sorrows and pain: 'The cure for pain is in the pain. Good and bad are mixed. If you don't have both, you are not a human being.'

Figure 22: The Rumble in the Jungle, the boxing match between Muhammad Ali and George Foreman, teaches us that we should not be afraid of feeling undesirable emotions if we aim to learn to deal with them. Just as pain is an inevitable part of a boxing match, anxiety, stress, and low mood are inevitable parts of life, and recognising this is part of the path of recovery from tinnitus distress.

So, what should we do if we feel anxious when we stop an avoidance behaviour while practising SEL? We should not fight the anxiety. We need to let it be. There are several thought experiments that can help us to gain a better understanding of how to deal with uncomfortable emotions and experiences:

1. Cool Swimming Pool (CSP): Let's imagine it is a hot summer day and you are by a cool swimming pool in the

afternoon taking a swimming lesson. In order to learn swimming skills, you need to get into the pool. Can you learn how to swim if you are afraid of water or wish to avoid getting wet? Can you avoid the water by trying to run over it? Perhaps you could run on the water if you had much stronger legs, bigger feet and the earth's gravity was also reduced. But in normal circumstances if you try to run on the water, you still will sink into it very quickly. So, to learn to swim, you need to get into the water and get wet. Once you start practising your swimming skills

Figure 23: Can you run on the water instead of swimming? Can you avoid getting wet during a swimming lesson? Submerging yourself in the water is a part of learning how to swim. Think of your emotions during an SEL experiment as being like the water in the swimming pool. We need to experience them to make progress.

in the pool you will realise that if you submerge yourself in the water, you will weigh less than the water that you displace, and this will lift you to the surface in seconds, without any effort on your part. This is a law of physics; on average your body is less dense than water, so you can float without effort. Once you have overcome your initial fear of submerging yourself, you can swim more effectively. Similarly, if you feel agitated, anxious or upset during exposure to a situation where your tinnitus is troublesome, you may want to get rid of these feelings immediately. But this is like wanting to avoid getting wet during a swimming lesson. When swimming you need to float in the water instead of avoiding it. You need to use the water to swim.

During the practice of SEL, you need to accept the anxiety, anger and irritation caused by hearing your tinnitus. Accept these emotions as part of your existence at that moment. You can reassure yourself that your anxiety and other negative emotions will subside as you progress with the SEL. There is no need for you to artificially remove the negative emotions. Remind yourself that the uncomfortable emotions that you are experiencing are related to the hormones adrenaline and noradrenaline, which are released into your bloodstream when you are in a stressful situation. These hormones increase your heart rate, blood pressure, sugar metabolism and oxygen level and produce other changes in your bodily functions, making you ready for a fight or flight response. It is not possible to fight chemical reactions within your body. You need to give them time to settle down. And they will settle down, based on the principles of chemistry and physiology of our body. It is the same as when we are submerged in water and are lifted up to the surface and float, based on the laws of physics. So, you need to remind yourself that, although these are unpleasant feelings, you do not need to get rid of them. Rather, let them run their course. Soon these hormones will be reabsorbed from your bloodstream and stored away safely for the next time that your body needs them. A patient asked, 'What if I get very angry and start throwing things, kicking and shouting?' The answer is that you would not do these things if you did not fear staying with the anger. Throwing things, kicking and shouting at people are actions that may be performed to reduce anger (pressure release). But if you don't aim to get rid of the anger then you won't end up doing these things and the anger will subside. The important lesson is to learn that you can feel angry and that's OK. Your emotions during the SEL experiment are like the water during a swimming lesson.

2. Pain in Rugby Training (PRT): The main purpose of this thought experiment is to establish what good we can see in a bad situation or in uncomfortable experiences/ emotions. Ask yourself whether the anxiety or other nega-tive emotions that you might be experiencing are normal human emotions or alien emotions. Most people would agree that feeling anxious, upset, irritated or angry are

common human emotions that we might experience when we are faced with unpleasant situations. Nevertheless, these are unpleasant emotions and none of us like to feel them. Naturally we would like to get rid of these feelings as soon as we can. However, the more we try not to have certain emotions the harder it becomes to dampen them down. Ask yourself if there is any benefit from feeling anxious, angry or irritated. What is the good in the bad? How can feeling the way that you do be of any benefit to you? Imagine that you are training to play rugby. You may feel a lot of pain during the training because people may push you, tackle you or bash into you. Most people consider pain as a negative sensation. But is there some good associated with feeling pain during rugby training? Well, for one thing, repeatedly feeling pain can improve your tolerance for pain. You may still feel the pain, but you can deal with it more effectively. For example, if the pain level is 55 per cent and your tolerance capacity is 30 per cent, you will be easily overwhelmed by pain. But if the pain remains at 55 per cent and your tolerance improves to 70 per cent, then you can cope with the pain. You still feel the pain and dislike it, but you are able to carry on doing what you need to do. So, the aim is not to stop feeling the pain, which is not possible unless you are numb. Rather, the aim is to tolerate the pain better. So, going back to tinnitus, ask yourself if there is any benefit in feeling anxious, angry or irritated while practising SEL. Is there some good in the bad? Can I avoid feeling anxious, angry and irritated throughout my life or is it inevitable that I will have these feelings sometimes? If the feelings are inevitable, then what is the benefit of feeling them during the practice of SEL? Well, just as when feeling pain during rugby training, feeling these negative emotions can improve your tolerance for them. If you are feeling irritated, this will improve your tolerance for being irritated and there is not much that you need to do to make it happen. So, you can use this concept to help you in accepting negative emotions. You can tell yourself that these are human emotions and are unavoidable, and by feeling them you will improve your tolerance for them.

3. Dark Spooky House (DSH): We often interpret our negative emotions as alarm signals. If we feel anxious, we may believe that we are in danger. If we feel angry, we may think that someone must have done something wrong. This hampers the process of accepting the negative emotions. The DSH thought experiment can help us to challenge this type of emotional reasoning with regard to tinnitus. Sometimes children are afraid of dark rooms. This can also be the case for adults. Imagine that you are trapped in an old, dark, spooky house and you feel very frightened. You cannot see anything clearly and perhaps you are afraid of some supernatural threat. Because you feel frightened, you experience bodily sensations related to anxiety and panic, and these may make you think that you are in immediate danger. But you may, in fact, be perfectly safe; there is no rational basis for believing that you are in immediate danger. Now imagine that before being trapped

Figure 24: *Believing that we are in danger makes us feel scared. What if our belief is not a true reflection of reality? Does feeling scared mean that we are in danger?*

in this dark, spooky house you had watched a horror movie about a haunted house. Would that make you feel more scared? And would it actually increase the danger? Most people would say that watching the film would make you more scared, but you would not actually be in more danger. So, if you are not in more danger, why would you feel more scared? Most people agree that feeling scared in this scenario does not mean that you are in danger. You are scared because of your thoughts, and your thoughts are influenced by your past experiences, your personality, your physical and mental health and your environment. See Step 6 to refresh your memory with regard to factors that influenced your tinnitus-related thoughts. To accept the negative emotions, you can tell yourself that feelings do not necessarily reflect reality. If I feel anxious this doesn't mean that I cannot cope with tinnitus.

All three thought experiments described here can help us to tolerate the negative emotions caused by exposure to tinnitus and by stopping avoidance behaviours and rituals.

An old proverb is 'no pain, no gain'. Sometimes it is easier for us to tolerate pain if we believe that it is worthwhile in the long term. And, knowing this, the pain does not necessarily result in anger, irritation and sadness. Here we introduce some new proverbs:

> No anger, no pleasure
> No sadness, no happiness
> No irritation, no delight

When we are no longer afraid of feeling uncomfortable emotions, we can learn from the opportunity that SEL provides and move on to practise SEL for a different behaviour. In Step 8, we will learn more about how to challenge our irrational beliefs by creating counter-statements, and how to use these techniques in managing our reaction to tinnitus.

We should continue with SEL until the fears are no longer relevant and then move on to the next behaviour from our exposure menu.

Step 8. Let the Sunshine in!

In Step 8 we focus on practising how to change our thoughts. One day, a twelve-year-old girl said: 'I like to push away the dark clouds and let the sunshine in with my positive thoughts'. She asked us to tell our other patients that 'Let the sunshine in' was her idea. So now we often tell our patients that negative thoughts are like dark clouds, and they need to blow them away and let the sunshine in.

In order to change our thoughts, we need first to appraise them. You should ask yourself:

- Is this thought really true? Think of your SEL. What were the thoughts that proved to be incorrect?

- Can I spot any of the ten common errors of judgement/ distortions in my thoughts?

- What are the advantages and disadvantages of thinking this way? For example, if I completely believed this thought, how would this lead to me to behave? Would this be helpful?

- Do I want to keep thinking this way?

- If I decide to change my thinking, can I do it?

If we decide that a negative thought is unhelpful or has some distortions or errors, we need to ask if we want to keep thinking this way or if we would prefer to modify the thought. If the decision is to change, we need to develop counter-statements that are alternatives to the negative thoughts. In CBT for tinnitus, counter-statements are used to neutralise negative tinnitus-related thoughts. Unlike the common perception, CBT is not about positive thinking, although positive thinking can help (see the chapter on Positive Psychology: CBT plus! on page 321). CBT is more about realistic and rational thinking. Thus, the counter-statements should be related to the negative thoughts without having the same errors of judgment (or thought distortions).

> CBT is not about positive thinking. CBT is more about realistic and rational thinking.

Please note that it is not expected that anyone will be completely rational or in control of their thoughts and feelings all the time. In fact, our shortcomings are important features that make us human. If we were completely rational all the time, there are many human emotions and qualities that we would not experience, such as love, sadness, excitement, carefreeness, vulnerability, bravery and selflessness. We would be like Mr Spock from *Star Trek*. There are lots of human virtues and desires that may not be rational but that are part of us. In our view, it would counterproductive to be rational at all times. CBT is about being able to break the vicious cycle of tinnitus distress by noticing and modifying some of our key troublesome thoughts. This can help us to minimise the distress caused by tinnitus. Once this happens, tinnitus loses its significance, and it is more likely that it will fade away into the background. To sum up, counter-statements should be related to negative thoughts without having the same errors of judgment. Counter-statements should be:

- relevant and contradictory to the corresponding negative thought

- positively worded (i.e. should not include a 'not', 'won't', 'don't')

- be in your own words

- be believable to you

- be simple

- should not imply an action: the counter-statement should not tell you to do something (e.g. you should not say 'I must relax' or 'I must focus on something else')

- be free from thought distortions (e.g. 'I will be able to sleep' although positively worded is jumping to a conclusion)

The table opposite gives examples of tinnitus-related negative thoughts and corresponding counter-statements.

Negative thoughts	Examples of counter-statements
I cannot fix my tinnitus. I have lost my problem-solving skills.	I can solve a lot of problems despite hearing tinnitus.
Tinnitus bothers me a lot and I cannot do anything about it.	Tinnitus is a challenging condition. I am living my life despite hearing tinnitus.
Because of my tinnitus I can no longer enjoy my life. I will always be miserable when hearing tinnitus.	Tinnitus is unpleasant. But there are lots of important things in life that I can enjoy despite hearing tinnitus.
Tinnitus makes me feel tired, therefore it is draining my energy.	My energy is used by all sorts of activities and organs within my body.

The negative thought 'I cannot fix my tinnitus. I have lost my problem-solving skills' is not really true. Although we may not be able to cure tinnitus, this does not mean that we have lost our problem-solving skills. The distortions in this thought are magnification and over-generalisation. There is no benefit in thinking this way. This thought doesn't give us any direction to go in to help ourselves. In fact, it is a dead-end thought that makes us feel hopeless. In contrast, the proposed counter-statement avoids the magnification and over-generalisation errors and is more consistent with reality. We know that we can solve problems on a day-to-day basis, either at work or in leisure situations, even when we hear loud tinnitus. The counter-statement 'I can solve a lot of problems despite hearing tinnitus' does not imply that the person can solve the mystery of tinnitus, but it also does not exaggerate the lack of problem-solving skills. In fact, being able to persevere and solve problems despite hearing tinnitus indicates persistence and capability. Pushing away the negative thought and thinking of the counter-statement can make us feel more confident and hopeful.

> Counter-statements should be relevant and contrary to the negative thoughts, positively worded, believable and, most importantly, free from thought distortions.

The thought 'Tinnitus bothers me a lot and I cannot do anything about it' is not entirely true. The fact that tinnitus bothers us a lot doesn't mean that we can't do anything about it. The distortions in this thought are discounting the positive and emotional reasoning. There is no advantage to thinking this way and it just makes us feel hopeless and irritated. The negative fact is that tinnitus can be a big life challenge, but the positive fact is that when we are challenged, we become stronger and learn more. We can also learn skills to minimise the impact of tinnitus and the bothersome thoughts that it can evoke. The counter-statement 'Tinnitus is a challenging condition. I am living my life despite hearing tinnitus' does not downplay the problems that tinnitus causes, but at the same time it does not ignore the positive fact that I am getting on with my life. In addition, the counter-statement does not take the emotion of being bothered by tinnitus as a sign of helplessness. Thinking of the counter-statement makes us feel that we are stronger than we anticipated.

The thought 'Because of my tinnitus I can no longer enjoy my life' is not true, because there are lots of things in life that we can enjoy despite hearing tinnitus. We can taste good food, enjoy the company of loved ones, be creative, exercise and so on. This thought has an all-or-nothing thinking distortion: either we have to enjoy everything or we will enjoy nothing. This is what the counter-statement needs to tackle. The counter-statement 'Tinnitus is unpleasant. But there are lots of important things in life that I can enjoy despite hearing tinnitus' acknowledges that tinnitus is unpleasant but also acknowledges the fact that we have the ability to enjoy things in life despite hearing tinnitus. This is comforting for us.

The thought 'Tinnitus makes me feel tired, therefore it is draining my energy' is a perfect example of emotional reasoning, which is characterised by thinking based on what our emotions seem to be telling us. Our energy is constantly being used by our muscles to maintain our posture against gravity (if they were not working, then we would be flat on the ground), our internal organs such as our heart are using energy to keep us alive, and our brains are using energy processing signals from our senses and planning actions. All these burn a lot of energy. So why should we single out tinnitus as draining our energy? In fact, every single cell within us uses energy. Tinnitus and our reaction to it also use energy but this is tiny compared with the energy consumed routinely by the body and brain. The counter-statement 'My energy is used by all sort of activities and organs within my body' offers a more balanced view and avoids the double standard of feeling that we can cope with the energy used by all sorts of bodily functions but not with the energy taken by tinnitus.

A common theme occurs when we are distressed by tinnitus, in which the uncontrollable persistence of tinnitus is worsened by our negative predictions and irrational thinking about it. In a way, the distress turns into suffering due to our own thinking pattern. As the Japanese writer Haruki Murakami said: 'Pain is inevitable, but suffering is optional'. This is consistent with the Buddhist metaphor of 'the second arrow'. The Buddha asks one of his students: 'How would you feel if you were struck by an arrow? Would it be painful?' The student says: 'Yes it would be painful'. Then the Buddha asks: 'What if you were struck by a second arrow?' Would it still hurt you? The student says: 'Yes, it would hurt even more'. The Buddha explains that the first arrow represents the challenges that life throws at us, and we cannot stop them. But the second arrow is self-inflicted. The second arrow is our reaction to the first arrow. In the context of this book, the first arrow is tinnitus, which is thrown at us by life and is out of our control. The second arrow represents our negative thoughts and behaviours in reaction to our tinnitus. The first arrow is painful, but it is the second arrow that disables us. CBT can help us to stop shooting the second arrow after the first one. Counter-statements are perfect examples of not shooting the second arrow and instead putting some natural remedies on the wound caused by the first arrow.

Figure 25: *Buddha teaches us that pain is inevitable, but suffering is a choice. Tinnitus is out of our control but whether we suffer from it or not depends on us.*

Now is the time to do some more practice. Have a go at developing counter-statements for these hypothetical negative thoughts using the worksheet on the next page.

Counter-statement worksheet

Negative thoughts	Write your counter-statements here
I cannot control my tinnitus or my feelings about it.	
Tinnitus makes me feel tired as I cannot sleep well at night. Tinnitus is a terrible disease with no cure!	
Tinnitus affects my sleep and concentration. Hence, it reduces my efficiency. I can no longer be in control at my workplace.	
Tinnitus invades every aspect of my life and makes me feel useless.	
I make a lot of mistakes because of my tinnitus.	
Tinnitus is like a fog that affects my performance.	

Below are the counter-statements that some of our patients were able to think of. Please note that these are just some examples. In CBT, you need to develop the skill of creating counter-statements of your own, statements that are believable to you and are reflections of reality based on the reality checks you have done while practising SEL.

The examples listed in the table below may not be believable or even true in your particular case. However, the examples may help you to develop the skill of generating counter-statements.

Counter-statement worksheet example

Negative thoughts	Examples of counter-statements
I cannot control my tinnitus or my feelings for it.	Most things in life are out of our control (e.g. the universe, organs in our body, traffic, weather). People survive and can feel happy despite the fact that most things in life are out of their control. Tinnitus is one among the big pile of the things in life that are out of my control. This is OK. However, there are helpful things that I can do to have some control over my feelings about tinnitus with the use of CBT skills.

Tinnitus makes me feel tired, as I cannot sleep well at night. Tinnitus is a terrible disease with no cure!	I am lying down and can rest despite hearing tinnitus. This is the second best compared to a deep sleep. Resting helps to energise me. Even if there is no cure, I can still live well with tinnitus.
Tinnitus affects my sleep and concentration. Hence it reduces my efficiency. I can no longer be in control at my workplace.	I can concentrate on my tasks most of the time. I can do whatever I need to do despite the difficulties caused by tinnitus. This makes me feel strong.
Tinnitus invades every aspect of my life and makes me feel useless.	Tinnitus is present most of the time and is a nuisance. Regardless of tinnitus, I can do whatever I need to do. This makes me feel useful.
I make a lot of mistakes because of my tinnitus.	I can do most things as well and accurately as I used to before I had tinnitus. It may take me slightly longer to complete my tasks. It is OK to double check my work for accuracy. My performance is intact despite tinnitus.
Tinnitus is like a fog that affects my performance.	I can see, hear and think even when I hear tinnitus loud and clearly.

You can use the Thought Analysis and Counter-Statement worksheet on page 246 to practise all the things discussed in this section. The first row is an example for you.

Thought Analysis and Counter-statement worksheet

Negative thoughts	Is this thought true? Is there any distortion?	What are the advantages and disadvantages of thinking this way?	How confident am I that I can change this thought, should I decide to do so? Rate from 0–10, where 0 means not confident at all?	My counter-statements
I cannot get rid of tinnitus and there is no way out. I am trapped.	I feel trapped because I cannot control tinnitus. But I do not feel trapped because I cannot control a lot of other things in life. This is emotional reasoning and magnification.	Thinking there is no way out or that I am trapped makes me feel depressed and panicky. There is no benefit in thinking this way.	I am 6/10 confident that I can change these. I have changed my mind many times in the past. I can do it now too!	There are lots of things that are out of my control, and I am OK with them. In fact, most things in life are out of our control. Despite this, people can live their lives happily.

After developing counter-statements for our negative thoughts, it can be helpful to put them in the Dark Cloud and Sunshine Worksheet. This worksheet can help us to memorise our negative thoughts and their corresponding counter-statements. In this way, in the heat of the moment, we can quickly remind ourselves of the relevant counter-statement to think about. After all, we need to be able to neutralise our negative thoughts within seconds, so knowing the counter-statements by heart can be very handy in implementing CBT. However, it is important to realise that CBT is not about having a good list of counter-statements; rather it is about mastering the skill of generating effective counter-statements. The worksheets introduced in this chapter can help us to practise this skill.

Dark Cloud and Sunshine worksheet

CBT is not about having a good list of counter-statements; rather it is about mastering the skill of generating effective counter-statements.

Step 9. Gloves Are Off! KKIS it (Know, Keep on, Identify and Substitute)!

The knowledge that we have gathered so far can assist us in the final task of CBT. This section provides an opportunity to put into practice the principles of CBT in managing tinnitus-related distress. In this section we introduce the process of Know, Keep on, Identify and Substitute with the acronym KKIS.

> KKIS provides an opportunity to put together everything that we have learned in Steps 1 to 8 in order to manage our tinnitus distress.

The first 'K' is to know when to do CBT. We need to do CBT whenever tinnitus interrupts our activities or affects our mood. Although you may hear your tinnitus all the time, it may not always cause distress or interrupt your activities. You only need to use CBT skills when your tinnitus is bothering you. To refresh your memory, see the section 'Recognising When to Do CBT' on page 153.

The second 'K' is to keep on with the negative emotions caused. For example, you may feel irritated or even panicky if you cannot do certain tasks due to your tinnitus. Here, you need to accept those negative emotions. Trying to push away the negative emotions is like trying to push away a pile of floating slime. If we try to push the slime away our hands will get stuck in it. Read the thought experiments starting on page 226 for ideas on how to accept our emotions (CSP, PRT and DSH). It is important to float in the water before starting to swim. Once we steady the ship and are not afraid of the emotions that we might be experiencing, then we are ready to move on to explore the reasons for our emotions and deal with them.

The 'I' is for identifying our thoughts. Review the THT worksheet on page 118 to refresh your memory about how to identify thoughts. Don't forget to identify a negative thought before thinking of a corresponding counter-statement. It is a common mistake for people to start thinking of random counter-statements whenever they are bothered by their tinnitus. This is like shooting in the dark and is less effective. The point is to neutralise the negative thought with a corresponding counter-statement. If you don't know what the negative thought is, then you can't generate a proper counter-statement.

The 'S' is for substituting our negative irrational thoughts with counter-statements. See Step 8 for practising counter-statements.

Whenever we are bothered by tinnitus, we need to use KKIS rather than seeking short-term relief. The KKIS process should be repeated every time tinnitus bothers us. This needs to be done at the time we are bothered by tinnitus, not retrospectively. You can use the KKIS worksheet to help you to practise this process. After you have practised KKIS several times using the worksheet, you can do it in your head without having to write anything down. After all, KKIS is a mental exercise. An example is given on page 254.

In the first column, write down what is happening when you are bothered by hearing your tinnitus. When is this? How loud is the tinnitus on a scale from 0 to 10? Where are you? Who are you with?

In the second column, write down what emotions you are experiencing and acknowledge that the emotions will subside on their own. Think that these are normal and common human emotions, and feeling them will improve your tolerance of them. You may spend about five to ten seconds thinking about these.

Most of your time is going to be spent filling in the third and fourth columns, which are the main CBT tasks. In the third column, write down what your thoughts are at the moment. What is the dark cloud? It is important to acknowledge that what you are writing down is not a literal fact but is your thought. In keeping with this, it might be a good idea to add 'I am thinking' before each thought that you write down in column three. Many of our patients say that by doing this, they immediately reduce the impact of the thought on their emotions. This is a technique borrowed from Acceptance and Commitment Therapy.

In the fourth column, let the sunshine in by thinking of a corresponding counter-statement! Each time you are bothered by tinnitus you need to make a new entry in the KKIS worksheet.

> KKIS is not aimed at getting rid of tinnitus or even our initial reactions/emotions to it. It simply helps us to acknowledge our reactions and stop them from snowballing by blowing away the dark cloud of negative thoughts and 'letting the sunshine in' by thinking of corresponding counter-statements.

Use the KKIS worksheet to practise your CBT skills.

254 • Living Well with Tinnitus

Know, Keep on, Identify and Substitute (KKIS) worksheet example

Know	Keep on	Identify	Substitute
It is 5 pm on Sunday. I am reading a book, and my tinnitus is 6/10. I can't concentrate. It makes me feel irritated.	I feel irritated. Irritation is a normal human emotion. It will run its course.	I am thinking 'I can never enjoy reading a book in silence.'	I can read and understand most of the text despite hearing tinnitus. This makes me feel confident that I can read and understand.
Monday 10:30 pm, I am doing a crossword puzzle before going to bed. My tinnitus is loud 9/10, which makes me feel frustrated.	I feel depressed. Depression is a common human emotion. It is there for a reason. It helps people to cope.	I am thinking 'I feel depressed. This proves that there is no way that I can get used to it and I am powerless.'	Feeling depressed is just an emotion. There are many things that can help me to get over tinnitus as well as depression.
Tuesday, 9 pm. I am watching TV and my tinnitus is loud 8/10 and is bothering me.	I feel irritation, annoyance and frustration. But this will build up my tolerance of these feelings. After all there will be many times in my life that I will feel these emotions (for	I am thinking 'Because I feel annoyed, my evening is spoiled.'	I am still able to enjoy the programme and concentrate reasonably well. I am learning how to manage tinnitus.

reasons other than tinnitus) so building up my tolerance to them is a good thing.				

Know, Keep on, Identify and Substitute (KKIS) worksheet

Know	Keep on	Identify	Substitute

Sometimes people may find it hard to KKIS. This is usually because they spend a lot of time doing things that are irrelevant to KKIS and by the time that they start to KKIS it is already too late. Let us explain this a bit more.

When we are at the first 'K', the exact moment when we realise that we need to do CBT, there is not much time to waste. In other words, we need to quickly start identifying the dark clouds and substitute them with sunshine thoughts, the 'I' and the 'S'. Of course, we should not jump the gun out of fear. That's when the second 'K' helps, as it provides a few seconds to reflect on the fact that our emotions can be accepted, and we don't need to fight them. All we want is to stop them from snowballing. Snowballing can happen due to our negative thoughts. Avoidance behaviours strengthen negative thoughts by preventing us from learning that the negative thoughts may not be true. Here we can use a thought experiment to understand this better. This thought experiment is called 'Who is Your Opponent?'

Imagine that you are a boxer, and you are waiting in the ring for the match to start. Three people catch your eye: your opponent, the referee and a spectator. How would you spread your focus on these three people once the match starts if you have ten 'units' of focus? How much of your focus should be on your opponent, how much on the referee and how much on the spectator? Remember that the total should be ten. Put the numbers that you think are appropriate in the spaces provided:

.... out of 10 on the opponent

.... out of 10 on the referee

.... out of 10 on the spectator

Most people give a high score for focus on the opponent, for example 9/10, but a low score for focus on the referee, say 1/10, and on the spectator, say 0/10. Now imagine you have ten resource units at a given moment that you can use for managing your tinnitus. When you are bothered by tinnitus, ask yourself, when you are at the first 'K' how many units of your resources should you use for dealing with your tinnitus (e.g. by trying to distract yourself from it), for accepting your emotions (the second 'K') and for changing your thoughts ('I' and 'S')? Remember that the total is ten. Write your answers below.

.... out of 10 on tinnitus

.... out of 10 on the emotions

.... out of 10 on identifying and changing thoughts

Instinctively, most people give a fairly high number to dealing with their tinnitus, for example 5/10. They usually give lower numbers to accepting emotions, say 2/10, and identifying and changing thoughts, say 3/10. But based on the CBT principles that we have learned in this book, devoting a lot of our resources to dealing with the tinnitus leads to a snowballing of our negative emotions. Instead, we should be focussing on accepting our emotions and identifying and changing our thoughts. Returning to the boxing example, imagine that your thoughts are the opponent, your emotions are the referee, and your tinnitus is a spectator. Imagine that when the match starts you devote 5/10 of your attention to the spectator, 2/10 to the referee and 3/10 to your opponent. What will happen? Yes, you will get knocked down. In fact, you will get knocked down very quickly. When the match starts, how much time do you have to work out who is your opponent and who is the referee or spectator? One minute? Twenty seconds? Or a fraction of a second? When you are at the first 'K' in KKIS, this is how much time you have to realise that you have to work on identifying and changing your thoughts, 'I' and 'S'. You cannot afford the time to focus your resources on alleviating your tinnitus. If you do, you will get knocked down very quickly by the punches of your opponent, your own thoughts. The next part of Step 9 helps us to add some depth to our CBT by digging deeper in our mind than just noticing automatic thoughts.

Identifying and resolving your cognitive conflicts

Cognition is a term that, broadly, means 'thought processes'. According to Aaron Beck there are three layers of cognition, comprising: automatic thoughts, rules of life and core beliefs. Figure 26 illustrates these cognition layers.

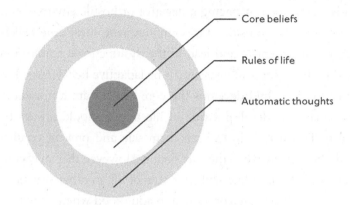

Figure 26: Layers of cognition according to Aaron Beck.

For people who suffer from anxiety, depression and other psychological disorders, automatic thoughts can become distorted. Cognitive distortions are systematic errors in logic derived from maladaptive attitudes or rules of life. During the course of cognitive development throughout life, individuals create various rules of life in order to regulate their emotions and behaviours. Rules of life are tied to an individual's core beliefs. Core beliefs are typically formed in childhood and are the deepest level of cognition. They include our most basic assumptions about our identity, the world around us and the future. Core beliefs are created based on our childhood interpretation of life events. Early life experiences lead to the development of positive core beliefs (e.g. 'I am good', 'I am worthy') and negative core beliefs (e.g. 'I am unlovable', 'I am incompetent').

Although some core beliefs appear dysfunctional and negative, they may have been adaptive for children during their early years when managing a negative or hostile environment. However, taken outside of this environment, these core beliefs become maladaptive and lead to the dysfunctional application of rules for living and consequent maladaptive behaviours. For example, if a child develops the core belief 'I am a nuisance', they may also develop a rule of life that 'I should always be quiet'. This may help to keep them safe and prevent conflict with their family when they are young. However, they may continue to behave in line with this rule of life in other situations and such beliefs may continue into adulthood where they may affect that person's relationships with other people. Positive core beliefs can promote the flexible application of rules of life and are likely to lead to a more realistic appraisal of threat. Having said this, some overly positive core beliefs can lead to problems. For example, over-confidence can lead to rash behaviour or narcissistic personality (an inflated sense of one's own importance).

In the context of CBT for tinnitus, our emotional reaction to tinnitus is explained in the following way. As an example, we may think that tinnitus affects our concentration and reduces our efficiency at work, thereby leading to the catastrophic conclusion that we will never work again to our own standards. This is an example of a negative automatic thought. But why do such negative automatic thoughts create anxiety in some people and not in others? This specific negative thought (I will never work again to my own standards) may violate rules and assumptions that we have established across our life span, such as 'In order to survive I should always be at peak efficiency'. These rules of life are in turn assumed to reflect a core belief (e.g. I am a failure). The onset of tinnitus can precipitate a perceived threat to these life rules. This leads to tinnitus-related anxiety and depressed mood.

Here are some examples of dysfunctional rules of life described by Aaron Beck:

- I should never feel hurt.

- I should always be happy and serene.

- To be happy I must be accepted, liked and admired by all people at all times.

- My value as a person depends on what others think of me.

- I should always be spontaneous.

- I should always control my feelings.

- I should never be tired or get sick.

- I should never hurt anybody else.

- I should always be at peak efficiency.

- If I make a mistake, it means that I'm inept.

- I should be a perfect lover, friend, parent, teacher, student and spouse.

The table of conflicts illustrates some negative automatic thoughts about tinnitus that violate some rules of life, leading to negative emotional reactions. This is based on the idea that the conflict between the negative automatic thoughts and the rules of life leads to our emotional reaction to tinnitus. It is important to reduce this conflict.

Recall that if tinnitus induces negative emotions, it is more likely to be perceived and to remain the focus of attention than if it does not evoke negative emotions. In CBT, the idea is to alleviate tinnitus-related distress by modifying the negative automatic thoughts as well as the dysfunctional rules of life.

Table of conflicts

This table shows the conflict between negative automatic thoughts and rules of life and the corresponding emotional reactions to tinnitus.

Negative auto-matic thought	Dysfunctional rule of life	Emotional reaction
I cannot fix my tinnitus. I have lost my problem-solving skills.	'I should be able to find a quick solution to every problem.'	Anxiety
Tinnitus bothers me a lot and I cannot do anything about it.	'I should never feel bothered.'	Hopelessness
Because of my tinnitus I can no longer enjoy my life. I will always be miserable when hearing tinnitus.	'I should always be happy and serene.'	Depression

Why me? I do not understand why I have tinnitus.	'I should know, understand and foresee everything.'	Anger
I cannot control my tinnitus or my feelings about it.	'I should always control my feelings.'	Irritation
Tinnitus makes me feel tired as I cannot sleep well at night. Tinnitus is a terrible disease with no cure!	'I should never be tired or get sick.'	Frustration
Tinnitus affects my sleep and concentration. Hence it reduces my efficiency. I can no longer be in control at my workplace.	'I should always be at peak efficiency.'	Disappointment
Tinnitus invades every aspect of my life and makes me feel useless.	'In order to be happy, I have to be successful in whatever I undertake.'	Irritation
I make a lot of mistakes because of my tinnitus. Tinnitus is like a fog that affects my performance.	'If I make a mistake, it means that I'm inept'	Anxiety

Based on CBT, if there is a negative core belief (e.g. 'I am use-less', 'I am unlovable') there will typically be rigid rules of life that aim to prevent the negative core belief from becoming true (Figure 27). Examples of such rigid rules are 'I must always be perfect at my work' and 'I must always be kind to others'. Breaking these rules will create a lot of anxiety. The perception of tinnitus can lead to negative automatic thoughts, such as *I cannot concentrate, therefore I cannot do my work properly* and *Tinnitus makes me short tempered, therefore I will be snappy with others*. These negative thoughts can break the rules of life and lead to the emergence of tinnitus-related anxiety, which in turn prevents the process of habituation. If there is a negative core belief such as 'I am not good enough', there may be rigid rules of life that aim to prevent this negative core belief from becoming true (Figure 28). Examples of such rigid rules are 'I must always avoid challenges' and 'I must always control everything'. Breaking these rules will create a lot of anxiety.

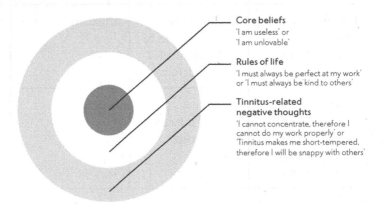

Core beliefs
'I am useless' or
'I am unlovable'

Rules of life
'I must always be perfect at my work'
or 'I must always be kind to others'

Tinnitus-related negative thoughts
'I cannot concentrate, therefore I cannot do my work properly' or 'Tinnitus makes me short-tempered, therefore I will be snappy with others'

Figure 27: Layers of cognition example.

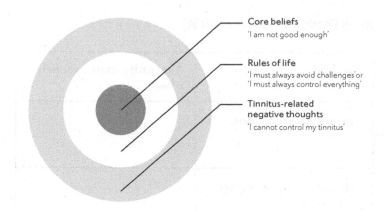

Figure 28: Layers of cognition example.

In order to give some depth to Step 9 of tinnitus self-management, we need to consider how we can modify our rules of life and core beliefs. The first thing that we can do is to develop alternative thoughts to neutralise the common dysfunctional rules of life, since the chances that we have some of them are high. After all, these are common!

Use the Rules Challenge worksheet (RCW) overleaf to suggest alternative more rational rules to replace these rules of life or perhaps make them more flexible.

Rules Challenge worksheet (RCW)

Rigid rules	Alternative more rational rules
I should never feel hurt.	
I should always be happy and serene.	
To be happy I must be accepted, liked and admired by all people at all times.	
My value as a person depends on what others think of me.	
I should always be spontaneous.	
I should always control my feelings.	
I should never be tired or get sick.	
I should never hurt anybody else.	

I should always be at peak efficiency.	
If I make a mistake, it means that I'm inept.	
I should be a perfect lover, friend, parent, teacher, student and spouse.	

Examples of alternative more flexible thoughts to replace the rigid rules that were given by some of our patients are listed in the RCW shown here:

RCW example

Rigid rules	Alternative more rational rules
I should never feel hurt.	Being hurt is an inevitable part of life.
I should always be happy and serene.	It is OK to have a wide range of emotions from sadness to happiness. This is only natural for humans.
To be happy I must be accepted, liked and admired by all people at all times.	I can be happy without being liked all the time. Happiness is an internal process and comes from how I think.

My value as a person depends on what others think of me.	I have value as a person regardless of what others think.
I should always be spontaneous.	Sometimes it is better to think twice.
I should always control my feelings.	It is OK to be spontaneous in how I feel.
I should never be tired or get sick.	Tiredness and sickness are a normal part of life. These help me to appreciate times when I feel lively and well.
I should never hurt anybody else.	It is inevitable that during my life people around me sometimes get hurt because of my actions. Most people will get over this.
I should always be at peak efficiency.	My efficiency can go up and down. This is normal.
If I make a mistake, it means that I'm inept.	Everyone makes mistakes. This provides further learning opportunities.
I should be a perfect lover, friend, parent, teacher, student and spouse.	The way that I manage my relationships with other people changes based on many different factors. How people feel about one another changes too.

We can use the new rules of life in some of our counter-statements. In this way we can change the negative thoughts and we make the rules that they are breaking more flexible and less likely to be broken in the future. For example, the thought *I make a lot of mistakes because of my tinnitus. Tinnitus is like a fog that affects my performance* is likely to break a rule that says, 'I must never make a mistake' or 'I must always be at peak efficiency'. Counter-statements for this negative thought could be 'I can concentrate enough on my tasks even when I hear tinnitus. Fog is different. There are many people who can concentrate on highly sensitive tasks despite hearing a lot of noise, for example, an architect in a building site or a pilot.' More flexible rules could be 'My efficiency varies from time to time, and this is normal' or 'Everyone makes mistakes, but mistakes provide learning opportunities.' Now we can combine the counter-statements in order to address the negative thought and the rule it might be breaking, all in one go: 'I can concentrate enough on my tasks even when I hear tinnitus. Fog is different. There are many people who can concentrate on highly sensitive tasks despite hearing a lot of noise, for example, an architect in a building site or a pilot. Anyway, my efficiency varies from time to time, and this is normal. Everyone makes mistakes, but mistakes provide learning opportunities.'

With regard to identifying core beliefs, we can use a technique called the Downward Arrow Technique. This involves first identifying what goes through our mind when we are distressed by tinnitus and then asking ourselves 'If my thought is true, what does this mean to me?' The Core Belief worksheet-Tinnitus

(CBW-T) can help you to identify core beliefs concerning you, the world around you and the future.

As shown in the example opposite, identifying core beliefs using the CBW-T involves several steps. As for some of the previous exercises, CBW-T starts with recognising the times when we are distressed by tinnitus. Then we need to identify what went through our mind at the time that our tinnitus was bothering us. These are the skills that we have already learned in the previous sections. Once we have identified our initial thought, we need to ask ourselves what this thought says or means about: (1) me; (2) the world around me; and (3) the future. We may need to repeat the questions several times. Each time we answer them, we get closer to our core beliefs. The core beliefs are usually very black and white absolute statements. They often are related to our childhood experiences.

Example of CBW-T worksheet

What is the event?
Tinnitus is distracting me from watching a TV show

What goes through my mind about my tinnitus?
Damn this noise, I can't enjoy watching TV.

What does that mean to me?
It means that I cannot enjoy anything because of this for the rest of my life.

Identifying Core Beliefs about Self	Identifying Core Beliefs about the World	Identifying Core Beliefs about the Future
If this is true, what does it mean about me? There is something wrong with me.	If this is true, what does it mean about the world around me or my life? My life is ruined. Why me?	If this is true, what does it mean about the future? I will never be able to have a normal life.
If this is true, what does it mean about me? I am a failure.	If this is true, what does it mean about the world around me or my life? Life is unfair.	If this is true, what does it mean about the future? The future is not good.

You can use the CBW-T in order to explore the deeper meanings behind your automatic thoughts.

CBW-T worksheet

What is the event?
....

What goes through my mind about my tinnitus?
....
....

What does that mean to me?
....
....

Identifying Core Beliefs about Self	*Identifying Core Beliefs about the World*	*Identifying Core Beliefs about the Future*
If this is true, what does it mean about me?	If this is true, what does it mean about the world around me or my life?	If this is true, what does it mean about the future? ....

If this is true, what does it mean about me?	If this is true, what does it mean about the world around me or my life?	If this is true, what does it mean about the future?
....	....	....
If this is true, what does it mean about me?	If this is true, what does it mean about the world around me or my life?	If this is true, what does it mean about the future?
....	....	....
If this is true, what does it mean about me?	If this is true, what does it mean about the world around me or my life?	If this is true, what does it mean about the future?
....	....	....

In order to modify our core beliefs, we need to think of alternative, more rational beliefs to replace the negative core beliefs. For example, 'I am a failure' reflects all-or-nothing thinking. Surely, we can come up with a more rational thought that is a better reflection of reality. Is this belief really true, based on our life experiences as an adult? Although it is not hard to imagine why a young child can develop a black and white belief of this type, based on the influence of their parents, peers or significant others, this most likely is not going to be appropriate for an adult's life. Most people agree that they must have achieved something during their life, so they cannot be a total failure. We all fail at many different things throughout life, but this doesn't mean that we are a complete failure. In fact, it is through failing that we learn. Often people come up with alternative thoughts, such as 'I am good enough.'

The next step is to list evidence in support of the new core belief. For example, think of five events based on your performance throughout life that would support the new core belief 'I am good enough'. As these core beliefs are formed in childhood, it is very likely that we have lots of examples of things that we have achieved throughout our life. For example: 'I have passed some of my exams', 'I have learned to ride a bike', 'I have helped . . .', 'I have worked . . .', 'I have been kind to . . .', and many more. When we create new core beliefs, we can use them in some of our counter-statements to add some depth to them. For example, in the CBW-T process you may discover that a negative thought *Because of my tinnitus, I will not be able to do my work properly* can be linked with a core belief

'I am a failure'. Therefore, you can create a counter-statement: 'I can complete my tasks to a reasonable standard even when I hear tinnitus. I am good enough.' Here we simply added the new core belief of 'I am good enough' to the counter-statement.

The Negative and Rational Core Beliefs (NRCB) worksheet can be used to list your core beliefs, develop alternative more rational beliefs, and write down the supporting evidence for your rational new core beliefs.

The NRCB worksheet here shows some examples of common negative core beliefs and alternative rational core beliefs that were developed by some of our patients during their therapy.

NRCB worksheet with example responses given by some patients.

Negative core belief	Alternative more rational core belief	Evidence for the new core belief
I am weak	I have both weaknesses and strengths	
I am vulnerable	Vulnerability is a part of all human beings	
I am a failure	I have had successes, so I am good enough	

I am unlovable	I can be loved	
I am unworthy	My worth and value as a person is always with me regardless of what I do or achieve	
I will be isolated	There is always someone who I can choose to communicate with	
Life is unfair	Life sometimes seems unfair. For me it has been more fair than unfair	
I am bad at everything	I can do some things well	

You may use the blank NRCB worksheet opposite to take note of your negative core beliefs, alternatives to them, and supporting evidence for your rational new core beliefs. The first row is completed as an example.

NRCB worksheet

Negative core belief	Alternative more rational core belief	Evidence for the new core belief
I am weak	I have both weaknesses and strengths	I can do many tasks. I can help others. I care about my family and or friends. I have achieved some goals in my life.

We need to incorporate what we have learned about rules of life and core beliefs into the KKIS process. This is not so difficult, but many of our patients found it hard to do. For this reason, we decided to elaborate on the process. There is no change in the first and second 'K'. The only real change that we need to make is to spend a bit more time on the 'I' and 'S'. Instead of just identifying the initial negative thoughts, we should speculate about what rules they are breaking and what core beliefs are related to them. Speculation about what rule is broken by a given thought will be largely based on comparing the negative thought with the list of common dysfunctional rules to see which of those could have been broken. Examples of the rules of life given earlier in this section provide a rough guide to identifying the rules that could have been broken due to some specific thoughts. Speculation about core beliefs will mainly be based on the work that we have done via the CBW-T. Opposite is an example of a KKIS that has been completed so as to incorporate counter-statements that challenge the negative thoughts, rules and core beliefs (the blank version of this table can be found on page 256).

Know, Keep on, Identify, and Substitute (KKIS) worksheet

Know	Keep on	Identify	Substitute
1-It is 5 pm on Sunday. I am reading a book, and my tinnitus is 6/10. I cannot concentrate. It makes me feel irritated.	I feel irritated. Irritation is a normal human emotion. It will run its course.	I am thinking 'I can never experience the pleasure of reading a book in silence.'	I can read and understand most of the text despite hearing tinnitus. This makes me feel confident that I can read and understand.
		Rule violated: I must always be happy.	We have a wide range of emotions from sadness to happiness and it is normal to feel them all.
		Core belief: I am a failure.	I am good enough.

2-Monday 10:30 pm. I am doing a crossword puzzle before going to bed. My tinnitus is loud, 9/10, which makes me frustrated.	I feel depressed. The fact that I feel depressed doesn't mean that I will not be able to cope with this. DSH: being scared doesn't mean that I am in danger.	I am thinking 'I feel depressed. This proves that there is no way that I can get used to it and I am powerless.' Rule violated: I should never get sick or tired. Core belief: I am weak.	Feeling depressed is a common human emotion. There are many things that can help me to get over this. Tiredness and sickness are a normal part of life. These help me to appreciate times when I am well. I have weaknesses and strengths

3—Tuesday, 9 pm.. I am watching TV and my tinnitus is loud, 8/10, and is bothering me.	I feel irritated, annoyed and frustrated. This will build up my tolerance for these feelings. I will get used to them.	I am thinking 'Because I feel annoyed, I will be snappy at my partner.'	I am still able to enjoy the programme and concentrate reasonably well. I am learning how to manage my tinnitus.
		Rule violated: I mustn't hurt anybody else.	It is inevitable that people around me get hurt at times, due to my actions or what I say. Most of the time they get over it soon.
		Core belief: I am unlovable.	I can be loved.

In the first entry of the KKIS example, one initial thought was *I can never experience the pleasure of reading a book in silence.* Let's assume that is true. Why does that matter to me? Perhaps it means that I cannot enjoy my life fully. Perhaps I believe that if I don't enjoy my life fully this means that I am missing out or failing. Perhaps I have a fear of failure. So, the initial negative thought in this instance may be related to the core belief 'I am a failure.' To avoid being a failure, I may think that I must always be happy, a rule of life. If I am happy, it means that I am a winner, but if I am not, I am failing. The combined counter-statement in the 'S' column addresses all these.

In the second entry, the initial thought is *I feel depressed. This proves that there is no way that I can get used to it and I am power-less.* This is an example of emotional reasoning. So, what is the problem here? It could be my resentment about being depressed or more generally resentment about being sick and tired. Of course, no one likes to be sick or tired. But these are facts of life, so why can't I just accept them and not be afraid? Maybe I am jumping to the conclusion that I will never be able to cope with being sick and tired, so I will never be able to get over my tinnitus. Maybe I am interpreting this as a sign of weakness and vulnerability. Now let's assume that I have a core belief that 'I am weak'. I see life events through the lens of this core belief. In other words, I am looking at the feelings of being depressed and powerless due to tinnitus through the lens of 'I am weak.' Therefore, it is understandable that I would interpret this as something that I cannot cope with. I may also believe that in order to survive I should avoid getting sick or tired, a rule of life. This rigid and unrealistic rule is of course broken by my initial thought.

Now my combined counter-statement gives me an alternative view that 'I have weaknesses and strengths.' So already I can look at the problem with a more balanced assumption. This matches well with the new rule that accepts the tiredness and sickness as facts of life. The new core belief also allows the counter-statement that accepts depression and accepts that there are solutions for it. This can also lead to a new belief, that it is strong to be open to looking for solutions and help. Unlike the contradictions between the initial negative thought and the rule, the counter-statement is complementary to the new rule. The importance of changing the rules and core beliefs is apparent in this example. If the rule is not changed, the counter-statement 'Feeling depressed is a common human emotion. There are many things that can help me to get over this' is still likely to break the old rule 'I mustn't get sick or tired.' The counter-statement may not be believable to me if I still look at the problem through the lens of my old core belief 'I am weak'.

In the third entry, the initial thought is 'Because I feel annoyed, I will be snappy at my partner.' This is another example of thinking based on our emotions and jumping to conclusions. So why does this thought bother me so much? What's the big deal if I snap at my partner? Surely, they understand that I am under a lot of stress due to my tinnitus. Surely my loved ones will empathise with me and try to calm me down. So, what does it mean to me if I snap at my partner? Maybe I think they will get mad at me. Maybe I think they will run out of patience with me. Maybe I think they will leave me. But why would they leave me if they love me? Maybe deep down I do not believe that they truly love me. Rather, I believe that I am unlovable, a core belief. I may also believe that to avoid being abandoned I should not hurt anybody, a rule of life. The initial negative thought breaks this rule and puts me in conflict with the core belief and its negative consequences. The combined counter-statement in the 'S' column gives me a different viewpoint, a new more flexible rule and a counter-statement.

It is important to remember that the aim of KKIS is not to remove the emotion that we experience at a given time. Rather, we need to acknowledge and accept our emotion (the second 'K') and stop feeding it by identifying and changing our irrational thoughts ('I' and 'S'). The emotions will then subside on their own. Imagine that you have a handful of snow (the emotions) in your hand. You accept the snowball and do not try to immediately melt it away. Perhaps you put the snowball on a plate to the side (the second 'K'). By identifying and changing your irrational thoughts (the 'I' and 'S') you make sure that the snowball doesn't grow. The ball of snow slowly melts away on its own.

Figure 29: *To practise KKIS we need to imagine that we have a handful of snow (the emotions/reaction to tinnitus) in our hand. We cannot magically make the snow disappear in an instant. Instead, we put it on a plate to one side. We can prevent the snow from accumulating by identifying and changing our irrational thoughts. Leave the handful of snow to melt on its own.*

Step 10. CBStyle: Integrating CBT into Our Lifestyle!

It should take us about two months to work through all the first nine steps introduced in this book. This period is called active treatment. After this period, the active part of the treatment comes to an end and we move on to the maintenance stage. Once the active treatment ends, we need to reassess our symptoms to monitor progress and to see if we have made improvements in managing our tinnitus. Self-assessment is very important because it can guide our next course of action. If we haven't improved enough in managing our tinnitus, either we need to go back to the active stage and practise more or we need to consider seeking professional help. If we have achieved what we set out to achieve and have become more confident in managing our tinnitus, it is OK to move on to the maintenance stage. The maintenance stage is very important, as it is during this stage that we have the opportunity to improve our ability and confidence in utilising CBT skills and managing tinnitus.

This is similar to graduating from courses such as medicine, engineering and law and starting work. As we gain work experience, we fully master and extend the knowledge and skills learned during our training. If, after graduation, we fail to find a job that gives us the opportunity to practise our skills, we may soon forget them, even if we were top of our class and graduated with distinction. Therefore, we need to plan to use our CBT skills for managing tinnitus after the active treatment stage. In other words, we need to integrate CBT into our lifestyle, as opposed to stopping using it once active treatment has ended.

However, it is important for our plan to be realistic. We need to allow for the possibility of setbacks and moments of weakness. In Step 10, we talk about the three components of the maintenance stage: 1) Self-assessment; 2) Integrating CBT into our lifestyle, called 'CBStyle'; and 3) How to deal with setbacks.

> It is important to be prepared for setbacks. They will happen, and if we are prepared for them, we can manage them and they will not escalate into a full-blown relapse.

1) Self-assessment

We can use the questionnaires in this section for self-assessment. The first two questionnaires can help us to evaluate the impact of tinnitus and hyperacusis on us. The third questionnaire is a screening tool for symptoms of anxiety and depression. The fourth questionnaire, called 4C, is a tool that helps us to re-evaluate our confidence in managing tinnitus and helps us to explore how to become more confident.

Tinnitus Impact Questionnaire (TIQ)

Over the last two weeks, how often would you say the following has occurred because of hearing a sound in your ears or head with no external source (e.g. buzzing, high-pitched whistle, hissing, etc.)?				
1. Lack of concentration	0–1 days	2–6 days	7–10 days	11–14 days
2. Feeling anxious	0–1 days	2–6 days	7–10 days	11–14 days
3. Sleep difficulties (delay in falling asleep and/or difficulty getting back to sleep if woken up during the night)	0–1 nights	2–6 nights	7–10 nights	11–14 nights
4. Lack of enjoyment of leisure activities	0–1 days	2–6 days	7–10 days	11–14 days
5. Inability to perform certain day-to-day activities/ tasks	0–1 days	2–6 days	7–10 days	11–14 days
6. Feeling irritable	0–1 days	2–6 days	7–10 days	11–14 days
7. Low mood	0–1 days	2–6 days	7–10 days	11–14 days

To calculate your total score, follow these instructions:

For each item, give yourself 0 points if you selected '0–1 days';
1 point if you selected '2–6 days'; 2 points if you selected '7–10

days'; or 3 points if you selected '11–14 days'. Add up the points for the seven items. This gives you your total score. How different is this from your pre-treatment score on page 73?

Hyperacusis Impact Questionnaire (HIQ)

Over the last two weeks, how often would you say the following has occurred because of certain environmental sounds that seemed too loud to you but people around you could tolerate well?				
1. Feeling anxious when hearing loud noises	0–1 days	2–6 days	7–10 days	11–14 days
2. Avoiding certain places because they are too noisy	0–1 days	2–6 days	7–10 days	11–14 days
3. Lack of concentration in noisy places	0–1 days	2–6 days	7–10 days	11–14 days
4. Unable to relax in noisy places	0–1 days	2–6 days	7–10 days	11–14 days
5. Difficulty in carrying out certain day-to-day activities/tasks in noisy places	0–1 days	2–6 days	7–10 days	11–14 days
6. Lack of enjoyment of leisure activities in noisy places	0–1 days	2–6 days	7–10 days	11–14 days
7. Experiencing low mood because of your intolerance to sound	0–1 days	2–6 days	7–10 days	11–14 days
8. Getting tired quickly in noisy places	0–1 days	2–6 days	7–10 days	11–14 days

To calculate your total score, follow these instructions:

For each item, give yourself 0 points if you selected '0–1 days'; 1 point if you selected '2–6 days'; 2 points if you selected '7–10 days'; or 3 points if you selected '11–14 days'. Add up the points for the eight items. This gives you your total score. How different is this from your pre-treatment score on page 77?

Screening for Anxiety and Depression in Tinnitus (SAD-T)

Over the last two weeks, how often have you been bothered by any of the following problems?				
1. Feeling nervous, anxious or on edge	0–1 days	2–6 days	7–10 days	11–14 days
2. Not being able to stop or control worrying	0–1 days	2–6 days	7–10 days	11–14 days
3. Little interest or pleasure in doing things	0–1 days	2–6 days	7–10 days	11–14 days
4. Feeling down, depressed or hopeless	0–1 days	2–6 days	7–10 days	11–14 days

To calculate your total score, follow these instructions:

For each item, give yourself 0 points if you selected '0–1 days'; 1 point if you selected '2–6 days'; 2 points if you selected '7–10 days'; or 3 points if you selected '11–14 days'. Add up the points for the four items. This gives you your total score. How different is this from your pre-treatment score on page 78?

A score of 4 or more indicates possible symptoms of anxiety or depression and indicates you should see your doctor for advice. Depending on your symptoms your doctor will let you know if you need to take any further action, e.g. seeing a psychologist or taking medication.

Finally, to assess how confident you are in managing your tinnitus, use the 4C questionnaire below.

4C Tinnitus Management Questionnaire

For each question, please select one number based on how you are feeling now.
1. How confident are you that you are able to carry out your day-to-day tasks, even with tinnitus? 0   1   2   3   4   5   6   7   8   9   10 Not confident at all   Very confident
2. How confident are you that you are able to rest and relax, even with tinnitus? 0   1   2   3   4   5   6   7   8   9   10 Not confident at all   Very confident
3. How confident are you that you can enjoy your life fully, even with tinnitus? 0   1   2   3   4   5   6   7   8   9   10 Not confident at all   Very confident

4. How confident are you that you can do all the above without using any avoidance behaviour?

0	1	2	3	4	5	6	7	8	9	10

Not confident at all   Very confident

To calculate your score for the 4C questionnaire, add the scores for the first three questions and multiply the result by the score for the fourth question. Then divide the result by three. This final number is your 4C score, expressed as a percentage (the maximum score is 100 per cent). How different is this from your pre-treatment score on page 160?

For the question asking, 'How confident are you that you are able to complete your day-to-day tasks even with tinnitus', what number did you give?

If you gave yourself 0, use the space below to write down your thoughts on why you gave yourself 0.

If you did not give yourself 0, use the space below to write down your thoughts on why you did not give yourself 0.

_____

_____

_____

_____

Now think what can help you to move to a higher number (unless you gave yourself 10 out of 10). What would you need to do differently to achieve a score of 10 out of 10 in being confident in completing your day-to-day tasks even with tinnitus? Use the space below to write down your ideas about what might help you to move to a higher number on this question:

_____

_____

_____

_____

For the question asking 'How confident are you that you are able to rest and relax even with tinnitus', what number did you give?

If you gave yourself 0, use the space below to write down your thoughts on why you gave yourself 0.

If you did not give yourself 0, use the space below to write down your thoughts on why you did not give yourself 0.

_____

_____

_____

_____

Now think what can help you to move to a higher number (unless you gave yourself 10 out of 10)? What would you need to do differently to achieve a score of 10 out of 10 in being confident that you can rest and relax even with tinnitus? Use the space below to write down your ideas about what might help you to move to a higher number on this question:

_____

_____

_____

_____

For the question asking 'How confident are you that you can enjoy your life fully even with tinnitus' what number did you give to yourself?

If you gave yourself 0, use the space below to write down your thoughts on why you gave yourself 0.

If you didn't give yourself 0, use the space below to write down your thoughts on why you didn't give yourself 0.

_____

_____

_____

_____

Now think what can help you to move to a higher number (unless you gave yourself 10 out of 10)? What would you need to do differently to achieve a score of 10 out of 10 in being confident that you can enjoy your life even with tinnitus? Use the space below to write down your ideas about what might help you to move to a higher number on this question:

_____

_____

_____

_____

The ultimate goal of tinnitus management based on CBT is to enable you to lead a normal, satisfying life without having to be dependent on avoidance behaviours or rituals. For the question 'How confident are you that you can do all the above without using any avoidance', what number did you give?

If you gave yourself 0, use the space below to write down your thoughts on why you gave yourself 0.

If you did not give yourself 0, use the space below to write down your thoughts on why you didn't give yourself 0.

_____

_____

_____

_____

Now think what can help you to move to a higher number (unless you gave yourself 10 out of 10)? What would you need to do differently to achieve a score of 10 out of 10 in being confident that you can manage your tinnitus without using any avoidance techniques? Use the space below to write down your ideas about what might help you to move to a higher number on this question:

_____

_____

_____

_____

Use the worksheet opposite to summarise your ideas on how to improve your tinnitus management (if you already have rated yourself as 10 out of 10, use the space below to take note of what has helped you to achieve this):

4C aspects	Your ideas on how to improve. If you rated yourself 10/10, what has helped you?
Confidence in completing day-to-day tasks even with tinnitus	In order to improve my confidence, I would need to . . .
Confidence that I can rest and relax even with tinnitus	In order to improve my confidence, I would need to . . .
Confidence that I can enjoy a satisfying life even with tinnitus	In order to improve my confidence, I would need to . . .
Confidence that I can do all of the above without using any avoidance	In order to improve my confidence, I would need to . . .

Use the worksheet overleaf to list your scores for the questionnaires that you completed during Step 2 (pre-treatment) and contrast them with your scores for the questionnaires that you completed during Step 10.

Worksheet for comparing pre- and post-treatment scores

Questionnaire	Step 2 (total score for each questionnaire <u>before</u> treatment using this self-help book)	Step 10 (total score for each questionnaire <u>after</u> treatment using this self-help book)
TIQ (page 73)		
HIQ (page 76)		
SAD-T (page 78)		
4C (page 160)		

If your Step 10 scores are less than 7 for the TIQ, less than 12 for the HIQ, less than 4 for the SAD-T and more than 52 per cent for the 4C, this indicates that you are probably ready to move on to the maintenance stage.

At present, there are no set changes in these questionnaire scores (the differences between scores in Stage 2 and Stage 10) that are defined as indicating a successful treatment outcome. Success also depends on your Step 2 score. The poorer your Step 2 score, the more room there is for improvement in Step 10. Conversely, the better your Step 2 score, the less room there is for improvement. What is your conclusion after comparing your Step 2 and Step 10 scores? Can you see any improvement? On a scale from 0 to 10, how ready are you to move on to the next stage? Use the space below to write down your reasons for being ready or what can help you to become ready if you feel that you are not yet there.

_____

_____

_____

_____

Based on the self-assessment, if your conclusion is that you are ready to move on to the maintenance stage, carry on reading this chapter. However, if your conclusion is that you are not satisfied with your progress and your scores are still high on the TIQ and HIQ, and low on the 4C, you may choose either to go back to the active stage and practise more or to seek professional help. Seeking professional help is even more important if your SAD-T score is above 4. Of course, if you have already sought professional help, this advice is not applicable.

2) CBStyle! Integrating CBT into our lifestyle

Some of the skills that we have learned in this book are introductory skills designed to prepare us to acquire the main skills of CBT. Therefore, we do not need to continue using the introductory skills beyond the practice that we have already done in the last few weeks. These were mainly preparatory steps towards learning the key CBT tasks - SEL and KKIS - that we need to carry on using. All the work that we have done during SEL has helped us to identify and minimise our avoidance behaviours and rituals. Once treatment is ended, it is important to accept tinnitus as opposed to using avoidance behaviours and rituals to escape from the uncomfortable feelings that it may cause. This means that SEL is an ongoing process. We may not need to practise SEL in the formal manner that we have learned in this book. Instead, we can use it based on our usual life scenarios. For example, if we find ourselves having an urge to avoid tinnitus by turning up the volume on the TV or by listening to background noise while working, or by drinking a special cup of green tea, we should *stop* these urges, *expose* ourselves to tinnitus and *learn* that we can do without any of these things. It is also useful to practise SEL in new situations. For example, if you are in a hotel room while on holiday and you feel the urge to use background noise to help you to sleep, use SEL. Practising SEL in different scenarios will help to strengthen and consolidate your skills.

Whenever we find ourselves being bothered by tinnitus, it is time to KKIS. In fact, simply *knowing* that we are bothered by tinnitus is the first part of KKIS. Next, we should *keep on* with that uncomfortable emotion for few seconds, and then *identify* our negative thoughts and *substitute* them with relevant counter-statements. At the start of the treatment, KKIS can take several minutes to do, but once we master this skill it can take only a few seconds to complete. Over time, the uncomfortable feelings that tinnitus might cause become less, and our tolerance for them increases, so dealing with them will take far less time. As Rumi said, tolerance and patience are developed if we see the eventual good results of an action, while intolerance is a sign of short sightedness, i.e. not being able to foresee the outcome and getting tangled up with negative predictions about what might happen. One way that SEL and KKIS help us is by providing the opportunity to see the outcome, hence improving our tolerance and patience. Recall the outcome from John's SEL experiment (Figure 20 on page 216). To minimise the impact of tinnitus on his sleep, he needed to face his fears. Once he stopped his avoidance behaviour, he learned that some of his anticipated difficulties were not as great as he feared. Learning this outcome helped him to improve his tolerance and to change his thoughts.

By practising, we will become more proficient in identifying our *hot* thoughts, so that we can identify them almost instantly. By using counter-statements on a regular basis and memorising them, they will come to us more naturally in a fraction of a second. Often, people get to a point where their negative thoughts are neutralised by counter-statements even before the negative thought is fully formed. In other words, they can stop the negative thought in its tracks and substitute it with a helpful counter-statement. We may not need to use the KKIS worksheet and instead do this purely mentally after treatment ends.

We need to make a lifestyle change of incorporating SEL and KKIS in our daily lives. It is like regular exercise. If we exercise daily and eat healthy food for six months and then stop, going back to old habits of low physical activity and junk food will mean that the strength and health that we gained during the six months of exercise and good diet will soon fade away. So, just as regular exercise and a good diet are essential for healthy living, SEL and KISS are essential for a healthy life with tinnitus.

> In order to keep our CBT skills sharply tuned for dealing with setbacks, we need to practise SEL and KKIS on a regular basis.

3) Dealing with setbacks

We also need to prepare for setbacks. Setbacks are part of our normal life, and if we are prepared for them, we can prevent them from escalating into a full-blown relapse. The likely causes of setbacks are: (1) our tinnitus getting louder or changing in some way or our hearing getting worse, and (2) stress and poor health.

Some of the factors that can lead to setbacks are avoidable and some are not. Hence, we need to be prepared for setbacks. Here we discuss the setbacks and what we can do about them.

1. Tinnitus can change for various reasons, many of which are unknown. Therefore it is not feasible even to try to stop it from changing. It is important to realise that changes in tinnitus usually do not mean that the problem that caused the tinnitus in the first place has become more severe. This

might be the case if tinnitus were a physical sound. For example, if your car engine makes a noise and the noise gets louder, this might be a sign of an engine malfunction. The noise that the car engine makes is a physical sound, i.e. it results in motion or vibrations of air molecules that travel from the source to your ears. If tinnitus were a physical sound, an increase in the loudness of tinnitus could mean that there is chance (not a big chance) that the underlying cause had got worse. This is sometimes true for rare cases of tinnitus caused by physical bodily sounds, such as blood flow. However, for most people, changes in tinnitus indicate nothing about the underlying cause. Tinnitus can get louder if we are in a very noisy place or in a very quiet place, or when we are feeling stressed or when relaxing, or when we are exercising in a gym or lying down in bed, having sex or not, and having a cup of coffee or not. The good news is that if tinnitus is perceived as louder, by using CBT skills we can ensure that the vicious cycle of distress is not formed or is broken quickly, which then provides our brain with a chance to put tinnitus into the background.

Of course, if we start taking a new medication and our tinnitus suddenly gets worse, we should discuss this with our doctor. In fact, it is a good idea to inform our doctor that we have tinnitus, so that they can do their best to avoid the use of medications that might aggravate it. However, if we start avoiding certain activities, foods or environments in the fear that tinnitus might get worse, we will simply end up limiting our lives. This is usually counterproductive, since the more we live our lives based on our fear of tinnitus worsening, the more important tinnitus becomes. When tinnitus becomes more important for us, our brain focuses on it even more, the very outcome that we are trying to avoid. This is why using SEL skills needs to be an ongoing process, even after treatment ends. SEL can strengthen our skills in dealing with changes in tinnitus.

Our hearing deteriorates as a part of the normal ageing process and because of exposure to intense sounds or chemicals that damage the ear. So it makes sense to avoid intense sounds in order to preserve our hearing. On the other hand, there is no need to avoid sounds that are unlikely to damage our ears. We need to look after our ears but not to turn ear protection into an avoidance behaviour or ritual.

The magnitudes of sounds are often specified using a measure called 'dBA'. When this measure is used, we refer to the magnitude of the sound as its 'level'. Sound level meters usually express the magnitude of sounds in dBA. Note that this is a physical measure and is not the same as the subjective loudness that we perceive. Roughly, the perceived loudness doubles each time the sound level is increased by 10 dBA. For example, an increase in sound level from 50 to 60 dBA results roughly in a doubling of loudness, while an increase from 50 to 70 dBA results in a four-fold increase in loudness.

How intense does a sound have to be for it to be potentially damaging to our ears? The answer depends on the duration of the exposure. We can listen to sounds at 70 dBA or lower for as long as we want, because they are not intense enough to damage our hearing. For most people, it is reasonably 'safe' to be exposed to continuous noise with a level of 85 dBA for eight hours over a 24-hour period. For every 3 dBA increase in exposure level, the acceptable exposure time is cut in half. The table overleaf shows the recommended time limit for different exposure levels without and with ear protection (e.g. ear plugs or earmuffs). The effective reduction in sound level produced by ear protection varies considerably depending on the type of protection and how well it fits. While the reduction can be as much as 30 dBA, we have conservatively assumed a reduction of only 10 dBA, because ear protection is often poorly fitted.

Sound level (dBA)	Example of the type of environment that can produce this sound level	Time limit without ear protection (per 24 hours)	Time limit with ear protection
85	Crowded restaurant with background music	8 hours	Safe all day
88	Noisy pub	4 hours	Safe all day
91	Maximum volume of some smartphones	2 hours	20 hours
94	Very noisy pub	1 hour	10 hours
97		30 minutes	5 hours
100	Pneumatic drill	15 minutes	2.5 hours
103		7.5 minutes	1.25 hours
106		Less than 4 minutes	37 minutes
109		Less than 2 minutes	19 minutes
112	Maximum volume of some smartphones, rock concert, chainsaw	1 minute	10 minutes
115	Disco, rave, extra loud rock concert	30 seconds	5 minutes
120 and above	Gunshots, fireworks at close range, explosions	No safe limit	Uncertain; can be unsafe even with ear protection

Sounds like rifle shots, mortars and explosions can produce very high momentary sound levels of 155 dBA or more. Without ear protection, such sounds can instantly damage our ears. Because of this, hearing loss is common among people who have performed military service, especially if they have seen active service.

With regard to using personal listening devices, we should limit our exposure to a total of forty hours per week for levels of not more than 80 dBA. The 'safe' limit is bit lower for children: the noise level should not exceed 75 dBA for forty hours per week. If you listen using a personal listening device in noisy situations, such as on a train or bus, it may be better to use insert earphones that seal the ear canal rather than over-the-ear headphones, because insert earphones are better at attenuating outside sounds, allowing us to keep the volume of our device lower. Even better, use noise-cancelling headphones or earphones. These include a miniature microphone to pick up background noise and use the microphone output to generate 'anti-sound' (like an inverted-polarity waveform of the noise), which partly cancels the background noise. If you go to rock concerts or discos regularly, you might consider investing in some 'earplugs for musicians'. These are special earplugs that reduce the sound level uniformly across a wide range of frequencies, thus avoiding the 'muffled' sound quality that occurs with conventional earplugs or earmuffs.

When our hearing deteriorates over time, our tinnitus

might get louder, but usually not by very much. The point that we need to pay attention to at this stage is that prolonged daily use of hearing protection in situations where the sound level is not potentially damaging is not recommended, because it can increase the risk that we become more sensitive to sound. Hearing protection should be used when the sound levels reach or exceed the safety limits shown in the table.

It is not uncommon for people to feel that they should protect their hearing to avoid making their tinnitus worse. This is why some people use hearing protection on a daily basis to prevent further hearing loss. This is a safety-seeking behaviour that is likely to contribute to further tinnitus-related anxiety. It is also common that people carry a sound level meter (or use their smartphone as a sound level meter) to measure the sound levels in different situations. This is mainly a ritual. As explained earlier, safety-seeking behaviours and rituals restrict our life experiences and are likely to contribute to tinnitus annoyance, making the tinnitus 'sound' even louder. Ongoing use of SEL can help us to overcome and prevent the development of these types of safety seeking and avoidance behaviours and to maintain effective tinnitus management. To sum up, we need to look after our ears but not to turn ear protection into an avoidance behaviour or ritual. It is important to see your audiologist or doctor if you feel that your tinnitus or hearing has changed. They can examine your ears and advise. If we find ourselves over-protecting our ears, ritualising sound level measurement and reassurance seeking, we need to practise SEL to deal with this.

2. A second type of setback is when tinnitus stays the same, but we become less tolerant of it, due to other life stressors. In other words, we may feel less able to cope if we are under a lot of stress due to work, relationships, finances, family matters or poor health. Although life stress cannot be totally avoided, we can certainly develop strategies to manage stress better. There are many stress-management resources available, and our doctor is in a good position to point us in the right direction. The 'Resources' and 'Further Reading' sections of this book list some possible sources of help with stress management. In addition, we may benefit from seeing a therapist (a mental health professional) to support our mental health in the same way that our doctor looks after our physical health. When we feel less able to cope with tinnitus due to the stresses of life, we need to take a step back and think about the factors that have led to our current reaction to tinnitus. We may go back to our TRS worksheet on page 187 and complete one based on the factors that are currently influencing our reaction to tinnitus. This can help us to put tinnitus in context and understand why our ability to cope with it has reduced. At times when we feel less able to manage our tinnitus, it becomes more important to implement KKIS. This is the main CBT skill that is designed to help us in difficult times. During a setback, we might need to go back to using the KKIS worksheet on page 254 as opposed to performing KKIS in our mind.

Summary of the Ten Steps

This section summarises the material presented in this book in ten practical steps that we need to take in order to manage tinnitus and overcome the challenges that it might present. The ten-step guide describes a coherent series of actions that we need to take when tinnitus is troublesome. The guide describes the knowledge that we need to gain and the CBT skills that we need to master in the journey of tinnitus management.

Step 1. Learn about tinnitus

When we experience tinnitus for the first time, it is important to see a physician, audiologist or otolaryngologist to assess our general health and to screen for any disorders of our ears and hearing system. This can help to ensure that tinnitus is not a symptom of a medical condition that needs treatment. In the rare cases when an underlying disease or medical condition is identified, treatment will be arranged. However, for most people, tinnitus persists regardless of any treatment that they might receive for the underlying condition. A more likely possibility is that the tinnitus is not associated with a known underlying disease or medical condition that needs to be treated. Therefore, management of the tinnitus is the next step forward.

Hearing loss is one of the most common conditions that coexists with tinnitus. Indeed, many researchers are of the opinion that tinnitus is associated with some form of damage to the ear or the auditory system, even when that damage is not revealed by conventional tests of hearing. If hearing loss affects your life, and you do not yet have hearing aids, then talking to your doctor or an audiologist about the use of hearing aids could be helpful. If you have hearing loss, hearing aids can help you to communicate with others in everyday life, thus reducing a possible source of stress.

One of the main stress-producing effects of tinnitus is fear of the unknown. There are many research studies demonstrating that education and enhancing knowledge about tinnitus is a very important step in tinnitus management, regardless of its cause. In summary, it is important to know what tinnitus is and what it can and cannot do.

Step 2. Self-assessment

It is important to self-assess our own symptoms. This can help us be more prepared when seeing a medical professional and it can also help us make up our mind about the help that we would like (if needed). For example, if you experience hearing difficulties (e.g. problems understanding speech in a noisy pub or restaurant) despite having had a hearing test and being told that your hearing is fine, you should ask an audiologist to perform more complex tests assessing your speech perception and your processing of auditory information. Self-assess your sensitivity to noise, hyperacusis and symptoms of anxiety and depression, using the questionnaires described in Step 2. Discuss the results of these with your doctor or audiologist and ask for advice.

Step 3. Learn about CBT

Before being able to use CBT, we need to do some preparatory work. We need to learn the principles of CBT and what it is intended to achieve. It is important to learn how tinnitus-related distress is conceptualised within the framework of CBT. If we can look at tinnitus distress through the lens of CBT, it becomes easier to realise how the problems caused by tinnitus can be managed using CBT. But to learn this we first need to understand the ABC model and the two-way interactions between our thoughts and our emotional reactions.

Step 4. Test the water!

Before fully committing to CBT, we need to test the water and try out some of the introductory skills that are needed to practise CBT. Only by testing the skills in real life scenarios can we make up our mind as to whether these are doable for us and whether they might be helpful. The main skills are tackling avoidance behaviours and rituals and facing our fears. Our fears will not stay with us forever if we face them. But they may stay with us for our entire life if we run away from them! We also need to practise identifying our key troublesome negative thoughts, known as *hot* thoughts. It is important to build the skill of being aware of what thoughts go through our mind and of evaluating them. This is not a skill that comes naturally to us, so we need to practise. Finally, it is important to know when to practise CBT. This is another prerequisite skill, because it helps to identify situations where CBT can help and to distinguish them from situations where CBT cannot help. Only by knowing these things can we make an informed decision as to whether or not to embark on CBT.

Step 5. Ready for the real thing?

You need to think whether CBT can offer what you would like to achieve. It is often the case that when we develop tinnitus, our first reaction is to want to get rid of it. This reaction is understandable and natural. However, CBT cannot help us with that. We may feel the urge to avoid tinnitus and to avoid any situations where our tinnitus might get worse. We may feel that we will not be able to have a fulfilling life if we cannot distract ourselves from our tinnitus. The CBT method is based on the exact opposite, which seems counterintuitive. In CBT, the only way out is through. Prior to engaging in CBT, we need to learn about it and think about our options. We need to consider whether CBT is the right path for us at this stage in our life and if we are able to engage in this process. You should think about how confident you are that you are able to carry out your day-to-day tasks, rest and relax, and enjoy your life even with tinnitus. Also, you should ask yourself how confident you are that you can do all these without using any distraction or avoidance. You should think about what can help you to become more confident in doing these things.

Step 6. Customise our treatment

Once we have decided that CBT is the right thing for us and have practised its introductory skills, it is time to customise the treatment. Everyone is different and there is no one way that tinnitus affects people. Use the template model in Step 6 on page 176 to describe your tinnitus distress. Write down your thoughts, emotions, bodily sensations and behaviours in the spaces provided in the template model. Think about which parts of this vicious cycle can be changed or modified. In addition to these things, use the TRS worksheet on page 187 to explore various personal and life factors that might have contributed to the reaction that you had to tinnitus in the first place. The TRS worksheet can help you to understand the reasons for your initial reaction to tinnitus and to accept that these reactions were inevitable given the circumstances that you were in and your personal factors. This will prepare you for embarking on the journey of modifying these reactions.

Step 7. Start to SEL!

SEL is an acronym for a CBT exercise in which we *Stop* our avoidance behaviours and rituals, *Expose* ourselves to tinnitus, and *Learn* from it. During the SEL exercise, we practise controlling our urges to use background noise or any other distractions or rituals when hearing tinnitus, we expose ourselves to what we are afraid of, and we learn that we can tolerate the uncomfortable feelings that tinnitus might produce. The preparatory work that we have done with regard to the exposure and ritual menus can feed into the SEL exercise. It is vital that we avoid using the main CBT skills (Steps 8 and 9) out of fear. Imagine again what would happen if a boxer rushed into using their best punches at the start of a boxing match in the fear of not being able to tolerate pain if they were punched by their opponent. Pain is inevitable in boxing and the boxer needs to accept this. Once they accept it, they can conserve their resources, box more strategically and improve their chances of winning. Similarly, once you go beyond the fear of being hurt by tinnitus, then you can strategically use your resources and win the game. The only way to become more tolerant of the negative feelings that tinnitus might cause is to experience them and learn about the outcome. Simply by experiencing anxiety, irritation and sadness you will improve your tolerance of them. In this way, you will not rush into using the final skills of CBT in the fear of not being able to tolerate uncomfortable feelings. Instead, you will go beyond the fear of experiencing negative emotions and use CBT skills to stop the vicious cycle of tinnitus distress. Think again of these newly made proverbs: No anger, no pleasure. No sadness, no happiness. No irritation, no delight.

Step 8. Let the sunshine in!

Step 8 requires practice in creating counter-statements that are used to neutralise the effect of negative tinnitus-related thoughts. This is not an easy task since counter-statements need be related to the negative thoughts without having the same errors of judgement (or thought distortions). Many of our patients have stated that creating counter-statements is the most difficult task in CBT. There are certain criteria that effective counter-statements need to satisfy. They need to be: relevant and contradictory to the corresponding negative thought; positively worded; in your own words; believable to you; short, simple and easily remembered. It is in this step that we practise blowing away the dark clouds of negative thoughts and letting the sunshine in with our rational counter-statements.

Step 9. Gloves are off! KKIS it!

Now is the time to put together everything that we practised throughout the previous steps and to break the vicious cycle whenever tinnitus is bothering us. Breaking the vicious cycle has the consequence that although we hear tinnitus it doesn't cause distress. When this happens, tinnitus loses its significance, and it is more likely for it to fade away into the background. Step 9 involves an ongoing process called KKIS (*Know, Keep on, Identify and Substitute*) that we need to practise whenever tinnitus bothers us. This involves *Knowing* when to do CBT, which is whenever tinnitus interrupts our activities or affects our mood. Then we need to *Keep on* with the negative emotions and to realise that we can live with them. Once we are not afraid of our uncomfortable emotions, we are ready to move on to *Identifying* our negative thoughts about tinnitus and *Substituting* them with counter-statements. We can also go deeper and revisit some of our rigid rules of life, our basic beliefs about ourselves, life in general and the future. This can give more depth to our tinnitus management programme.

Step 10. CBStyle

The final step is to integrate CBT into our lifestyle (CBStyle). This is the maintenance stage. It is important to self-assess and decide if we are ready to move on to the maintenance stage. During the maintenance stage, we should expect setbacks and be prepared for them. To be ready to deal with setbacks, we need to keep using SEL and KKIS. In this way, we won't feel overwhelmed by the setbacks, and we can again use SEL and KKIS to break the vicious cycle of anxiety whenever it develops.

Positive Psychology: CBT Plus!

The aim of this chapter is to help us develop acceptance of the experience of tinnitus. It may be hard to accept tinnitus because there is nothing nice about it. The idea of this chapter is to use the power of positive psychology to generate optimism, which is important for improving mental health. We learned in the past chapters that we all experience thought distortions, which can include a tendency to focus more on negative experiences, discount positive experiences and over-generalise negative thoughts in relation to ourselves, others and the future. It can be helpful to remind ourselves of our strengths and what we are doing well, to try to find a more realistic, balanced perspective. Research studies have shown that realistic optimism is one of the qualities that makes people resilient. Resilience is a critical factor that can help us in developing the willingness to live life to the full even with tinnitus.

Our brain habituates to most steady sounds so that we become unaware of them after some time. In principle, the same thing can happen for tinnitus. However, we do not habituate to sounds that are emotionally significant or that indicate danger. Similarly, tinnitus-related anxiety and annoyance prevent the natural process of habituation. There are several research studies indicating that the processing of emotionally significant stimuli in the brain is enhanced in comparison with the processing of neutral stimuli. This means that when tinnitus induces negative emotions, such as anxiety, fear, annoyance, anger or guilt, it is more likely to be perceived and to remain the focus of attention than if it does not evoke negative emotions. We need to develop acceptance and willingness to live our life to the full even with tinnitus.

> Our brain cannot habituate to tinnitus as long as there are emotional obstacles.

Acceptance in this context means acknowledging the presence of tinnitus without attempting to change or stop it. Obviously, most people who experience tinnitus do not wish to have tinnitus and have a great desire to get rid of it. This is a very natural human reaction to unpleasant feelings or situations. As there is no definitive 'cure' for tinnitus or a known reliable method to reduce it, the desire to avoid or stop tinnitus is considered an unfeasible goal. Setting out to avoid or reduce tinnitus and failing to do so is likely to lead to the development of self-defeating cycles of negative thoughts and feelings and behaviours that hinder the process of habituation. This negative cycle can be broken if we accept ourselves as we are, including our tinnitus, and by using more flexible ways of managing it (for example, with the use of the CBT skills described in this book).

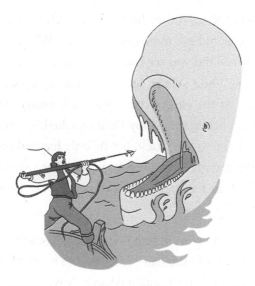

Figure 30: *The story of* Moby Dick *by Herman Melville (1851) is a good example of the catastrophic consequences that can result from a lack of ability to accept something that cannot be changed.*

Let's remind ourselves of one of the greatest American novels, *Moby Dick* (1851), by Herman Melville, a masterpiece of symbolism about an eccentric old whale-hunting captain named Ahab. He hunted an especially large species of whale. One of the whales that he had come up against was the legendary Moby Dick, pure white and more ferocious than any whale Ahab had seen before. In their first encounter, Moby Dick bit off Ahab's leg and wrecked his ship! Ahab was lucky not to die. He was sad that he had lost his leg but soon that sadness turned to anger, and that anger turned to madness. He wanted to kill Moby Dick so badly that he recruited a new crew and set off to hunt for Moby Dick. When he met other captains, he only asked them if they had seen the White Whale. If they said yes, he would ask more questions like 'Where did you see him?' or 'When did you see him?' But if they said that they had not seen the White Whale, he would just say goodbye and be on his way. At the end of the story, Ahab finally came across Moby Dick once again. Moby Dick attacked his ship and his crew urged him to turn back, but he only focused on trying to capture the monster. As a result, his ship was destroyed and Ahab and all of the crew died except for one, Ishmael, who lived to tell the story.

The moral of this story is that if you attack something that you can't defeat, out of pure hate, you will lose in the end. It would have been sensible for Captain Ahab to leave Moby Dick alone and get on with his life. But clearly the thought of Moby Dick and the emotions evoked by Moby Dick stayed in Ahab's head and drove him to behave in a reckless way.

It is only natural to want to get rid of tinnitus. To some people, developing a willingness to live with tinnitus means being defeated. It is only reasonable to aspire to do whatever you can to help yourself and to get rid of an irritating condition like tinnitus. We have had some patients who took years to realise that the path of acceptance was the way forward. After all, it is really up to you! Would you prefer to spend your time and resources finding ways of dampening down your tinnitus? Or would you prefer to have the opportunity to lead a satisfying life with tinnitus? If the former, then we respect your choice. If the latter, this book is intended to help you.

But how can we be willing to live our life with tinnitus? What can help us to achieve this? You might be surprised if we tell you that in our opinion there is little or nothing that you can do to help you to fully accept your tinnitus, in the sense that you think it is perfectly OK. Some people try to make tinnitus a positive thing by telling themselves 'tinnitus is my friend' or 'tinnitus proves that I am alive'. However, this way of thinking seldom actually helps people to fully accept their tinnitus. Even when we try to think of tinnitus in a positive way, it feels somewhat artificial.

Although it may be difficult to fully accept tinnitus, it is much more achievable to aim to accept 'you' as you are. In other words, you may accept the whole person that you are, including tinnitus, instead of trying to accept tinnitus without acknowledging the wider context. So, the question is: 'Am I acceptable to me?'

Don't fight Moby Dick! We need to develop willingness to live our life with all its positive and negative aspects, instead of trying to accept tinnitus in isolation.

So far, we have talked about how tinnitus can cast a negative shadow on our lives. In contrast, in this section the focus is on exploring positive aspects of our lives. This can help to build a full picture of us at this stage in our life, so we can decide whether 'I' am acceptable to me. So, what are the positives of life? Money? Friends? Happiness? Comfort? Good food? What is it that we should take into consideration to build a full picture of us? Positive psychology suggests that for the pursuit of optimism we should search from within and notice our own built-in strengths and virtues instead of trying to find something positive external to us. This is consistent with Rumi's idea that if you wish to see the sun, don't turn away from it and don't look at the shadows. Of course, the shadows may be a sign of the sun's presence but they don't tell us much about the sun itself. If we want to explore the positive aspects of our lives, we should not get distracted by focusing on our health, wealth, happiness, social network, comfort, etc. These are like the shadows. Instead, we should look more closely to find our intrinsic worth.

According to Peterson and Seligman, there are six common human strengths and virtues, as listed below:

- Temperance

- Transcendence

- Wisdom and knowledge

- Courage

- Humanity

- Justice

In this chapter, we explore our strengths and virtues as well as doing some positive psychology experiments.

Temperance

Temperance is defined as voluntary self-control. For example, we may avoid taking revenge by invoking our forgiveness and mercy, we may prevent ourselves from being self-important by exercising modesty, we may be prudent instead of reckless, and we may avoid greed by sharing with others.

How much of the following do you have within you? Choose a number between 0 and 10.
Ability to forgive 0   1   2   3   4   5   6   7   8   9   10 None   The most possible
Prudence (practicality, being sensible) 0   1   2   3   4   5   6   7   8   9   10 None   The most possible
Modesty (not boastful) 0   1   2   3   4   5   6   7   8   9   10 None   The most possible
Self-control 0   1   2   3   4   5   6   7   8   9   10 None   The most possible

Use the space below to write down for each of the above characteristics why you chose a certain number and the reasons
why you did not give 0. If you gave 0, think if this truly reflects
how you have behaved throughout your life. For example,
have you really never forgiven anyone? If you have forgiven
someone, then you have the ability to forgive within you and
we suggest that you go back and re-enter your scores. If after
reflection you still think that you are at 0 for a particular characteristic, then use the space below to write down what might
help you to move from 0 to a higher number.

Ability to forgive

_____

_____

_____

_____

_____

Prudence (practicality, being sensible)

_____

_____

_____

_____

_____

Modesty (not boastful)

_____

_____

_____

_____

_____

Self-control

_____

_____

_____

_____

_____

So overall, how much 'temperance' do you think that you have?

If you were going to put a price tag on this quality, what would it be?

Exercise

This exercise is one of the positive psychology interventions that is designed to increase your optimism by identifying and appreciating your key strengths.

The exercise is very simple. Use the space below to write down your five most pronounced strengths. Then write down a few ideas about how you could use these strengths more often over the course of the next week. Then follow this plan for one week.

_____

_____

_____

_____

_____

_____

_____

_____

_____

_____

_____

Transcendence

Transcendence means 'going beyond' or 'extending or lying beyond the limits of ordinary experience'. Examples of this virtue are having hope, spirituality, humour, gratitude and appreciation of beauty and excellence.

How much of the following do you have within you? Choose a number between 0 and 10.
Hope 0   1   2   3   4   5   6   7   8   9   10 None   The most possible
Spirituality (religiousness, faith, purpose) 0   1   2   3   4   5   6   7   8   9   10 None   The most possible
Gratitude 0   1   2   3   4   5   6   7   8   9   10 None   The most possible
Appreciation of beauty and excellence (awe, wonder, elevation) 0   1   2   3   4   5   6   7   8   9   10 None   The most possible
Humour 0   1   2   3   4   5   6   7   8   9   10 None   The most possible

Use the space below to write down for each of the above characteristics why you chose a certain number and the reasons why you did not give yourself 0. If you gave yourself 0, think if this truly reflects how you have been throughout your life. For example, have you never been grateful to anyone, or have you never laughed at a joke? If you think on reflection that you did sometimes feel grateful or you did sometimes laugh at a joke, then we suggest that you go back and re-enter the scores. If you think your score really is 0 for a particular characteristic, use the space below to write down what might help you to move from 0 to a higher number.

Hope

_____

_____

_____

_____

Spirituality

_____

_____

_____

_____

Gratitude

_____

_____

_____

_____

Appreciation of beauty and excellence

_____

_____

_____

_____

Humour

_____

_____

_____

_____

So overall, how much 'transcendence' do you think that you have?

If you were going to put a price tag on this quality, what would it be?

Exercise

Use the space below to write a letter of gratitude to a person who has been kind to you, but who you have never properly thanked. If you would like to, you can then post the letter or deliver it in person.

_____

_____

_____

_____

_____

_____

_____

_____

_____

_____

_____

_____

_____

_____

Some people choose not to do the exercises. This is very understandable, as they may be feeling overwhelmed by their tinnitus, the distress it causes and perhaps lack of sleep. They may feel hopeless and not convinced that carrying out the assignments can make any difference. Of course, there are many people who do choose to complete these exercises and feel that these are crucial to the success of therapy. Research shows that people who complete the exercises improve more than those who do not. Would you like to improve the management of your tinnitus and enjoy your life fully despite hearing tinnitus? If your answer is yes, then you should complete the exercises provided here.

Wisdom

Wisdom means the quality of having life experience, knowledge and good judgement. The qualities under this category comprise: creativity, curiosity, open mindedness, love of learning and having perspective.

How much of the following do you have within you? Choose a number between 0 and 10.										
Creativity (originality, ingenuity)										
0	1	2	3	4	5	6	7	8	9	10
None									The most possible	

Curiosity (interest in new things, openness to new experiences)										
0	1	2	3	4	5	6	7	8	9	10
None										The most possible

Open-mindedness (willingness to consider alternative points of view, critical thinking)										
0	1	2	3	4	5	6	7	8	9	10
None										The most possible

Love of learning										
0	1	2	3	4	5	6	7	8	9	10
None										The most possible

Perspective (wisdom)										
0	1	2	3	4	5	6	7	8	9	10
None										The most possible

Use the space below to write down for each of the above characteristics why you chose a certain number and the reasons that you did not give yourself 0. If you gave yourself 0, think if this truly reflects how you have been throughout your life. For example, have you ever solved a puzzle or wondered how a gadget works? If so, you have some curiosity, and we suggest that you go back and re-enter your scores. If you think your score really is 0 for a particular characteristic, use the space below to write down what might help you to move from 0 to a higher number.

Creativity

_____

_____

_____

_____

_____

Curiosity

_____

_____

_____

_____

_____

Open-mindedness

_____

_____

_____

_____

_____

Love of learning

_____

_____

_____

_____

_____

Perspective

_____

_____

_____

_____

_____

So overall, how much 'wisdom' do you think that you have?

If you were going to put a price tag on this quality, what would it be?

Exercise

Make a note of three things that went well each day for a week because of a wise or sensible thing that you did. Include what you did to bring this good thing about.

Day of the week	What went well?	What did I do to bring this good thing about?

Courage

Courage means strength in the face of pain or grief. Courage means that you can be brave and carry on despite being in danger. It also means that you can be genuine and reveal your true self, even if this might not be flattering.

How much of the following do you have within you? Choose a number between 0 and 10.										

Authenticity (the ability to be genuine and truthful)

0	1	2	3	4	5	6	7	8	9	10
None										The most possible

Bravery

0	1	2	3	4	5	6	7	8	9	10
None										The most possible

Persistence (perseverance, industriousness, the ability to continue in the face of adversity)

0	1	2	3	4	5	6	7	8	9	10
None										The most possible

Vitality (zest, enthusiasm, vigour, energy)

0	1	2	3	4	5	6	7	8	9	10
None										The most possible

Use the space below to write down for each of the above characteristics why you chose a certain number and the reasons that you did not give yourself 0. If you gave yourself 0, think if this truly reflects how you have been throughout your life. For example, have you ever managed to complete a difficult task? If so, you have some persistence. We suggest that you go back and re-enter your scores. If you think your score really is 0 for a particular characteristic, use the space below to write down what might help you to move from 0 to a higher number.

Authenticity

_____

_____

_____

_____

_____

Bravery

_____

_____

_____

_____

_____

Persistence

_____

_____

_____

_____

Vitality

_____

_____

_____

_____

_____

So overall, how much 'courage' do you think you have?

If you were going to put a price tag on this quality, what would it be?

Exercise

Use the space below to write about incidents in your life that show you at your best. Review the story daily over the next week and consider which of your strengths were involved.

What incident showed me at my best?		
	Which of my strengths helped me to perform the way I did?	How can those strengths in my character help me to cope with tinnitus?
Day 1		
Day 2		
Day 3		
Day 4		
Day 5		
Day 6		
Day 7		

Humanity

Humanity is the quality of being humane, able to love, being kind and being socially intelligent.

How much of the following do you have within you? Choose a number between 0 and 10.		
Love (having the capacity to love something or someone) 0 1 2 3 4 5 6 7 8 9 10 None The most possible		
Kindness (generosity, nurturance, care, compassion, altruistic love and niceness) 0 1 2 3 4 5 6 7 8 9 10 None The most possible		
Social intelligence (ability to judge how other people are feeling and to predict what they will do) 0 1 2 3 4 5 6 7 8 9 10 None The most possible		

Use the space below to write down for each of the above characteristics why you chose a certain number and the reasons that you did not give yourself 0. If you gave yourself 0, think if this truly reflects how you have been throughout your life. For example, have you ever supported a charity or shared your food? If so, then you have some kindness. We suggest that you go back and re-enter your scores. If you think your score really is 0 for a particular characteristic, use the space below to write down what might help you to move from 0 to a higher number.

Love

_____

_____

_____

_____

_____

Kindness

_____

_____

_____

_____

_____

Social intelligence

_____

_____

_____

_____

_____

So overall, how much 'humanity' do you think you have?

If you were going to put a price tag on this quality, what would it be?

Exercise

Ask somebody that you trust to list what they think are your most important strengths.

Use the space below to write them down. Use one of them in a new and different way every day for a week.

Day of week	My strength	How did I use it today?

Justice

Justice is fairness in the way that people are treated. Social responsibility (citizenship), fairness and leadership are among the aspects of justice.

How much of the following do you have within you? Choose a number between 0 and 10.
Citizenship (social responsibility, loyalty, teamwork) 0   1   2   3   4   5   6   7   8   9   10 None   The most possible
Fairness 0   1   2   3   4   5   6   7   8   9   10 None   The most possible
Leadership 0   1   2   3   4   5   6   7   8   9   10 None   The most possible

Use the space below to write down for each of the above characteristics why you chose a certain number and the reasons that you did not give yourself 0. If you gave yourself 0, think if this truly reflects how you have been throughout your life. For example, have you ever made sure that each person gets a share of the food at a picnic? If so, then you have some fairness. Have you ever found a lost item and handed it in to the police?

If so, you have some citizenship. We suggest that you go back and re-enter your scores. If you think your score really is 0 for a particular characteristic, use the space below to write down what might help you to move from 0 to a higher number.

Citizenship

_____

_____

_____

_____

_____

Fairness

_____

_____

_____

_____

_____

Leadership

_____

_____

_____

_____

_____

So overall, how much 'justice' do you think you have?

If you were going to put a price tag on this quality, what would it be?

Let's put our virtues and character strengths on one side of a set of scales and tinnitus on the other. Which side is heavier? Tinnitus may bother us a lot, and be a heavy weight, but on reflection we may greatly enjoy possessing these strengths and virtues, which may outweigh our tinnitus.

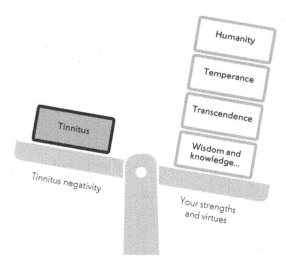

Figure 31: *Human virtues and character strengths on one side of a set of scales and tinnitus on the other.*

Final Words

It is often the case that when we develop tinnitus, our first reaction is to want to get rid of it, an entirely understandable reaction. However, CBT cannot help us with that. Our instinct may tell us to avoid tinnitus. We may feel that we will not be able to live a satisfactory life if we cannot distract ourselves from our tinnitus. As we have learned in this book, the CBT method is based on the exact opposite, a seemingly counter-intuitive path. In CBT, the only way out is through.

At first, we may think that CBT is about simply changing our negative thoughts and having positive thoughts instead. However, in the first section of this book we talked about the 1986 Woody Allen film *Hannah and Her Sisters*, which showed us the fact that our anxieties do not simply disappear if we try to be positive and reassure ourselves that we will be fine. Perhaps we may believe that we should push away our tinnitus distress by thinking about some good memories. Reading this book should have shown you that this hardly ever works. As Dante said in his *Divine Comedy* (1320): 'There is no sorrow greater than, in times of misery, to hold at heart the memory of happiness'.

To recover from tinnitus distress, we need to take a very systematic approach. This book helps us to achieve this by reviewing facts about tinnitus and how to assess our symptoms, by motivating and preparing us for behaviour changes, by teaching us the techniques of CBT, by helping us in developing the willingness to live a satisfying life even with tinnitus, and by facilitating learning using metaphors and thought experiments.

In this book, we have learned about the importance of building up our tolerance, using as an example Muhammad Ali's story of the Rumble in the Jungle. We learned how acceptance can change our life outlook using the example of *Beauty and the Beast*. From captain Ahab and Moby Dick, we learned not to waste our resources trying to do something that cannot be done. We learned from Buddha that if life injures us with one arrow, we should not make the situation more painful by further injuring ourselves with the second arrow. From Aristotle and Rumi, we learned that the philosophical underpinnings of CBT have strong roots in western and eastern cultures throughout the millennia and have passed the test of time. The thought experiment of 'You are the surgeon' helped us to understand how to focus on using CBT techniques correctly instead being distracted by ruminations about whether CBT will help us or not. We learned to imagine our distressing emotions caused by tinnitus as a ball of snow and to put that ball on a plate to the side. The ball of snow cannot be made to disappear in a few seconds, but it will melt on its own. We learned to focus our energy in stopping it from snowballing through challenging and modifying our tinnitus-related irrational thoughts.

The overall aim of this book is not to get rid of tinnitus. Rather it is to modify the thoughts, emotions and behaviours that lead to tinnitus distress by breaking the vicious cycle. From the thought experiment of 'Dark Spooky House', we learned that if we are feeling scared this does not necessarily mean that we are in danger, and we learned that we should not interpret what our emotions seem to be telling us as literal facts. This book is based on CBT, but presents a specific type of CBT, using techniques that have been proven to be successful and that have led to high patient satisfaction in our tinnitus clinics.

Figure 32: 'Now I feel confident to blow away the tide (tinnitus distress)!' *These were words from one of our patients who completed audiologist-delivered CBT for tinnitus.*

In conclusion, we are reminded of what one of our patients said in his last CBT session. He is the patient we mentioned in the introduction who felt like being a hopeless lonely shrimp in the sea which was about to be swamped by the deadly waves of a tsunami. At the end of therapy, he no longer felt that way. He said:

> After the therapy I feel stronger, braver and more positive. It is inspirational. Previously, I had been experiencing this tide, this huge tsunami of negativity, suffering, pain, anguish and everything, right from the time that my tinnitus started. Now I feel confident to blow away the tide! I feel that we are mounting the forces of good, riding the horses of the cavalry, charging into it and saying: no! I don't need to avoid my tinnitus. Instead, I can use CBT to control my reaction to it, a change from within!

> Nevertheless, I feel that I need to become more confident before the therapy comes to a close. You are not going to like this, but I think I need more sessions with you! I feel a bit like I am being told: you've got all the tools that you need now – go off and use them, baby! This makes me anxious.

It is completely understandable to feel anxious about how to continue implementing CBT skills and to think that we need ongoing support. However, it is important to emphasise that CBT is designed to be a time-limited therapy, and once we have completed the course, we need to become more independent in utilising CBT skills in our daily life and continuing the journey of learning.

Let's finish this book with a poem by Hafez of Shiraz, the most prominent fourteenth-century Persian poet:

For many years my heart was in search of Jamshid's cup
Searching and asking strangers for what was inside me

In Persian mythology Jamshid was a king and Jamshid's cup was a cup of divination, similar to the Holy Grail of Western culture. In this poem, Hafez expresses the idea that people keep looking for Jamshid's cup in many places, but they miss the fact that the cup lies within them. In the other words, the solution to our problems is within us. We just need to find it. This is very much the case for the management of tinnitus. The solution for coping is within us. We know what it feels like to experience tinnitus. We know our fears and weaknesses. We also know our strengths and motivations. We know what experiences we had in the past and what challenges we have overcome throughout our lives. We know what helped us and what didn't. The CBT methods described in this book are simply aimed at guiding us in the right direction. But we need to take the initiative and recruit all our internal resources to help us on the journey of recovery. We need to own the skills described in this book and use them in our own unique way that suits us. In managing tinnitus, the most important person who can help you is you!

Resources

Internet cognitive behavioural therapy (iCBT) for tinnitus management

www.icbt4tinnitus.com

Samaritans (a charity providing emotional support to anyone in emotional distress, struggling to cope or at risk of suicide throughout the United Kingdom and Ireland)

www.samaritans.org

British Tinnitus Association

www.tinnitus.org.uk

American Tinnitus Association

www.ata.org

Tinnitus Research Initiatives

www.tinnitusresearch.net

International Conference on Hyperacusis and Misophonia

www.hyperacusisresearch.co.uk

The British Psychological Society

www.bps.org.uk

American Speech-Language-Hearing Association

www.asha.org

American Academy of Audiology

www.audiology.org

British Academy of Audiology

www.baaudiology.org

British Society of Audiology

www.thebsa.org.uk

International Society of Audiology

www.isa-audiology.org

Safe listening devices and systems: a World Health Organization (WHO) standard

www.who.intpublicationsiitemsafe-listening-devices-and-systems-a-who-itu-standard

U.S. Environmental Protection Agency, Office of Noise Abatement and Control

www.epa.gov

Further Reading

Aazh, H., Bryant, C. and Moore, B.C.J. (2020). 'Patients' perspectives about the acceptability and effectiveness of audiologist-delivered cognitive behavioral therapy for tinnitus and/or hyperacusis rehabilitation'. *American Journal of Audiology*, 28: 973–985.

Aazh, H., Landgrebe, M., Danesh, A. et al. (2019). 'Cognitive behavioral therapy for alleviating the distress caused by tinnitus, hyperacusis and misophonia: Current perspectives'. *Psychology Research and Behavior Management*, 23:991–1002.

Aazh, H, and Moore B.C.J. (2018). 'Effectiveness of audiologist-delivered cognitive behavioral therapy for tinnitus and hyperacusis rehabilitation: Outcomes for patients treated in routine practice'. *American Journal of Audiology*, 27:547–558.

Baguley, D., Andersson G., McFerran, D. and McKenna, L. (2013). *Tinnitus: A Multidisciplinary Approach*: New York, John Wiley & Sons.

Beck, J.S. (2011). *Cognitive Behavior Therapy: Basics and Beyond*. New York: The Guilford Press.

Beukes, E. W., Andersson, G., Manchaiah, V. and Kaldo, V. (2021). *Cognitive Behavioral Therapy for Tinnitus*. USA: Plural.

Fuller, T. , Cima, R., Langguth, B. Mazurek, B. Vlaeyen, J.W. and Hoare, D.J. (2020) 'Cognitive behavioural therapy for tinnitus.' *Cochrane Database of Systematic Reviews*, 1: CD012614.

Harris, R. (2019) *Act Made Simple: An Easy-to-Read Primer on Acceptance and Commitment Therapy*. USA: New Harbinger Publications.

McKenna, L., Baguley, D. and McFerran, D. (2021) *Living with Tinnitus and Hyperacusis*. UK: Sheldon Press.

Remenyi, J. *Rock Steady: Healing Vertigo or Tinnitus with Neuroplasticity* (2020). Canada: Page Two.

Index

References to figures appear in italic type

and SEL 226
thought experiments
226–33
tolerance 318
APD Guide (Campbell) 40
appreciation of beauty and
excellence *331*, 333
Aristotle *93*, 94
audiological evaluations 31
auditory canal 42
auditory nerve 42
auditory processing disorder
(APD) 40
auditory system
abnormal neural activities
35
damage to 36, 39, 44, 314
early stages 42
aural fullness 42
authenticity *340*, 341
automatic thoughts 89, 190–2
avoidance behaviours *see also*
background music
and acceptance 135–6,
136–7
and CBT 70, 315–16
dependence on 50
dominating lives 63
exposure menus 141, *142–3*,
145–6
human instinct 132
and hyperacusis 43
overcoming 138–9, 138–47,
217

and rituals 4–5, 62–3
and SEL 302
strengthening negative
thoughts 258
avoiding tinnitus 63
awareness 126–7

B
background music 4, 46,
62–3, 131, 133 *see also*
avoidance behaviours;
listening to podcasts
background noise 215
Baguley, David 38
Beauty and the Beast
(Villeneuve) 12–13,
134–5, *135*, 352
Beck, Aaron 94, 192, 260–1,
261, 263
Beck, Judith 190
bedtime rituals 50, 211, *212 see
also* rituals
Beliefs/underlying thoughts (B,
ABC model) 95–104, 191
see also ABC model
biased thinking 194–5 *see also*
mental filtering
blame 197–8
bodily noises (somatosounds)
34
bothersome thoughts 238
boxing 14, 224–5, *226*,
258–60, 318
brain 92

OVERCOMING

Mild Traumatic Brain Injury and Post-concussion Symptoms

A self-help guide
using evidence-based
techniques

an
OVERCOMING
publication

O

NIGEL S. KING

Overcoming Mild Traumatic Brain Injury

(Available now)

Up to 10 per cent of people will suffer a mild head injury (or 'mild traumatic brain injury') in their lifetime and up to 50 per cent of those people will also find they have lingering post-concussion symptoms in the months or years afterwards. These symptoms can include headaches, dizziness, fatigue, irritability, sleep disturbance, reduced day-to-day memory, poor concentration, taking longer to think, 'muzzy' headedness, depression, anxiety, tinnitus, blurred or double vision, sensitivity to light or noise, frustration, nausea, restlessness and sensitivity to alcohol. In such circumstances the 'mild' head injury may feel anything but mild. This is particularly so if large areas of your day-to-day life are affected.

Complicating factors can make it very difficult to find the right kind of service or expertise after a TBI. Patients can easily feel like they are being 'pushed from pillar to post' when trying to find services that can help with their problems. On top of all of this, there is a distinct lack of good, science-based information for patients about the best ways to manage PCS. It is therefore very common for those who experience prolonged difficulties to find their situation extremely confusing, frustrating and stressful.

Dr Nigel King is an expert with much experience in this area, and has written a very valuable book weaving together the most useful knowledge in this area. It clarifies some of the complex issues for those who suffer with prolonged problems and provides practical, science-based self-help guidance for managing TBI difficulties. Using cognitive rehabilitation techniques and CBT approaches for the associated mental health complications of PCS, this much need book provides help, hope and understanding for what can be a highly disabling and misunderstood condition.

OVERCOMING
Chronic Pain

2nd Edition

A self-help guide
using cognitive
behavioural techniques

an
OVERCOMING
publication

FRANCES COLE
HELEN MACDONALD
CATHERINE CARUS

Overcoming Chronic Pain

2nd Edition

A self-help guide using cognitive behavioural techniques

(Available now)

Take control of your life, take control of your pain

Chronic pain can be extremely debilitating; however, it does not need to dominate your life. This self-help book is based on highly effective self-help methods developed by specialists and used in community and hospital pain management programmes. Your experience of pain can be greatly reduced by pacing daily activities, reducing stress, learning relaxation techniques and effective ways to cope with depression, anxiety, worry, anger and frustration.

This easy-to-follow book sets out:

- Why pain can persist when there's no injury or disease present
- How to become fitter and pace your activities
- Practical ways to improve sleep and relaxation
- Tips for returning to work, study and gaining a life you value

Overcoming self-help guides use clinically proven techniques to treat long-standing and disabling conditions, both psychological and physical.

This book is recommended by the national **Reading Well** scheme for England delivered by The Reading Agency and the Society of Chief Librarians with funding from Arts Council England and Wellcome.

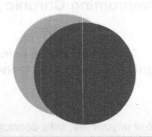

OVERCOMING
Insomnia
2nd Edition

A self-help guide
using cognitive
behavioural techniques

an
OVERCOMING
publication

O

COLIN A. ESPIE

Overcoming Insomnia

2nd Edition

A self-help guide using cognitive behavioural techniques

(Available now)

*All the help you need to conquer your
sleep problems and start living life to the full*

Poor sleep is one of the most common health problems and can leave you feeling exhausted, stressed and run down. While prescribed medications and over-the-counter remedies rarely offer lasting benefits, cognitive behavioural therapy (CBT) can help.

This essential self-help book is written by one of the world's leading insomnia experts and uses CBT strategies to help you to overcome sleep problems – including persistent insomnia – and to enjoy your life once again.

It includes advice on:

- Developing good pre-bedtime regimes
- The most effective relaxation techniques
- Establishing a new sleeping and waking pattern
- Dealing with a racing mind
- Using sleeping pills more effectively
- Handling jet lag and sleepwalking

'I sped from sceptic to full fangirl'
Mariella Frostrup, presenter of
The Truth About Menopause, BBC

Living Well
THROUGH
THE
Menopause

An evidence-based cognitive behavioural guide

OVERCOMING

**MYRA HUNTER
AND MELANIE SMITH**

Living Well Through the Menopause

(Available now)

An essential book to help women to live well through the menopause and to cope effectively with menopausal symptoms, using a cognitive behavioural therapy (CBT) approach.

Living Well Through the Menopause is based on a wealth of research, including randomised controlled trials of the MENOS intervention with over 1000 women, that has demonstrated the effectiveness of this approach specifically for menopausal symptoms – hot flushes, night sweats and also their impact on daily life. CBT is proven as an effective alternative for women who do not want or are unable to use hormone therapy (HT).

Written in an accessible and interactive style, with case examples and quotes, this guide will empower you and, specifically:

- Help you to understand and cope with your physical and emotional reactions to the menopause
- Clarify your key goals, thoughts and feelings using interactive questions and homework sheets
- Enhance your self-care through behaviour change
- Help partners and loved ones to support you through the menopause